YUKON QUEST

YUKON QUEST

The Story of the World's Toughest Sled Dog Race

Lew Freedman

Alaska Book Adventures™
EPICENTER PRESS

Epicenter Press is a regional press publishing nonfiction books about the arts, history, environment, and diverse cultures and lifestyles of Alaska and the Pacific Northwest.

Publisher: Kent Sturgis
Acquisitions Editor: Lael Morgan
Editor: Rhesa Bubbel
Proofreader: Melanie Wells
Cover & text design: Victoria Michael, Michael Design
Printer: Thomson-Shore

Cover photos: Front cover composite top photos of Bob McAlpin and two frosty dogs, Larry and BoyCuz, Copyright ©2010 by Carol Falcetta; bottom photo Copyright ©2010 by Eric Engman; back cover photo of Yukon River scene Copyright ©2010 by Eric Engman.

About the photo on page 6: There was a big crowd in Whitehorse in February, 2009 as mushers left at three-minute intervals to start the long, cold run to Fairbanks.

Library of Congress Control Number: 2009943407
ISBN 978-1-935347-05-7
10 9 8 7 6 5 4 3 2 1
Printed in the United States of America

To order single copies of this title, mail $14.95 plus $5.00 for shipping (WA residents add $1.90 state sales tax) to Epicenter Press, PO Box 82368, Kenmore, WA 98028; call us at 800-950-6663, or visit www.EpicenterPress.com.

DEDICATION

To Alaskans and Yukoners, whose enterprising,
can-do attitudes enable events like the Yukon Quest
that express the spirit of the North

CONTENTS

ALASKA BOOKS BY LEW FREEDMAN

ACKNOWLEDGEMENTS

A big thank-you to all of the mushers and officials who spent time talking with me about an event they love. And a special thank-you to those who went beyond the call of duty with their help: Bob Eley, Roger Williams, LeRoy Shank, John Firth, Tania Simpson, Stephen Reynolds, Dee Enright, Wendy Morrison, and my wife, Debra, who indulges my interests and is a first-rate transcriber.

INTRODUCTION

In the same manner that basketball is king in Indiana and hockey is paramount in Montreal, racing sled dogs is the sport of Alaska and primary entertainment of the Yukon. There are only two 1,000-mile (1,609-kilometer) sled dog races in the world — the Iditarod Trail Sled Dog Race and the Yukon Quest International Sled Dog Race. The Iditarod, first run in 1973, starts in Anchorage, Alaska's largest city, and runs to Nome each March. The Quest, first run in 1984, alternates directions between Fairbanks and Whitehorse each February.

Despite many similarities, these two races differ. Frequently, temperatures on the Quest are colder, the trail has fewer checkpoints, and there's more distance between checkpoints. Some believe the Quest is the toughest race on the face of the earth. In truth, in any given year, the weather dictates whether that is reality.

What is indisputable is that the Yukon Quest is a special event, a competition that boggles the thoughts of the sedentary, piques the curiosity of the inquisitive, tickles the senses of the adventurous, and defies the comprehension of those who instinctively curl up in extra blankets with the first dusting of snow.

The Quest has provided a fresh pantheon of northern heroes — men and women who have accomplished the improbable and succeeded in taming, if only briefly, the snowy, windy, and icy elements that all residents of the Far North know so well be it frostbite, frozen cars, or roads as slick as a skating rink. To many, those symptoms of winter are loud warnings to stay home. To Yukon Quest mushers, they are an undeniable call to adventure.

PROLOGUE

The terrain is some of the harshest and most beautiful in North America. Mountains are covered with ice and snow, the land is dotted with spruce trees, and it takes a special person to appreciate its raw loneliness and the removal from civilization, and to cope with the months-long darkness and intense cold.

The vast and empty swath of land comprising Alaska's Interior and Canada's Yukon Territory is reserved for the rugged and the romantic, the bold, the independent and the centered self, not the self-centered. It is the land of dreamers and of rich traditions. This is a place the intrepid choose in winter. They do not fear temperatures dropping to -50 Fahrenheit (-46 Celsius). For the strong-minded the Far North's extremes offer an affirmation that they are alive. For the weak-minded, it is the wrong place to be.

In 1896, word of a new gold discovery in the Yukon spread around the world, attracting thousands of men and a few women from as far away as England and Australia.

The newcomers, most arriving in summer, were exhilarated at first. They found a fresh, untamed frontier and a sun that lit up the sky at midnight. It was an unexplored land open to all comers, a place literally rich in possibility and adventure. Every day, miners waited anxiously to register their claims, standing among a hundred others, jawing about which outfitter had the best deal on gold pans. Yes, at first, it was exciting — chasing the fever, adopting a new lifestyle, and hacking out a place in the frontier. But month after month of picking through pebbles and silt, finding just enough gold to eke out a living, wore on a man's will.

Just as summers are beautiful and fertile, winters are harsh and barren. For weeks on end, the weather remained severely cold, no matter whether you measured the temperature in Fahrenheit or

Celsius. It was a cold that made your breath hesitate. Frost gathers on your eyelashes and your hands ache despite two layers of mittens. Dark "days" consist of eighteen hours of starry skies, and rivers are as solid as the ground you walk on. There is no escaping the long winter.

During the cold months, some earned a living trapping and others provided transportation to the small settlements that sprang up along the Yukon River and elsewhere. Mail and supplies had to be hauled in. The best mode of transportation was dog sled travel.

In bitterly cold weather, spit freezes before hitting the ground, mechanized equipment seizes up, and even the air refuses to move. But a sled dog will keep pulling. Trappers used the sled-and-dog combination as an efficient and reliable way to travel. The dogs were able to pull heavy weight even on the poorest trail. These dogs were an important part of a unique tradition preserved in literature by Jack London, in poetry by Robert Service, and in reportage by Pierre Berton. Those gold-rush dogs were the historic ancestors of the "canine athletes" that race across Alaska and the Yukon today.

The Yukon Quest is a story of international cooperation. There is a boundary separating Alaska and the Yukon, but for those who survive and thrive in winter, the line is artificial. There is more of a kinship than a difference.

Mike Laforet, a one-time gold miner, historian and Yukon gadfly, said the Far North captures the mind. "It stimulates the imagination," he said. "Alaska and the Yukon, they're brother and sister." Alaska and the Yukon are the fresh-start corners of the United States and Canada, retreats from the pace and the rules of the big city. "Cities have people," Laforet said. "Northern places have opportunity. You have the chance to be somebody else. It's like the frontier of the Old West."

That piece of wisdom was true in Gold Rush days and it is true now. A number of the modern-day immigrants to Alaska and the Yukon are dog-mushers. In a sense, the Iditarod and the Yukon Quest, like Alaska and the Yukon, are brother and sister. But they are not twins. It is frequently colder on the Quest, often windier on the Iditarod. The Iditarod passes through more populated villages and the Quest travels through more remote land. For many of the best mushers in the world, the call of the wild to attempt racing both of them is nearly irresistible.

The boldness of spirit may be what we admire most in dog mushers and the way they coax brilliant performances from their athletic animals who love to run. Northern fame has been manufactured on the trail, household names created, mushers revered for their achievements. As a past champion and veteran of twenty-four Yukon Quest races, Frank Turner is probably the most famous athlete in the Yukon. And it has been shown that anyone who has the championship of a Yukon Quest race on his resume is a dog driver to be respected and admired. Lance Mackey, a four-time winner, conquered cancer and then proved how tough his ravaged body was by conquering the Quest.

The Yukon Quest is definitely a place to come if you have something to prove to yourself, or to the world. There will come a time and a place along the trail when the body is weakening, the cold is penetrating the bones, visibility is non-existent because of blowing snow, when the dogs and musher would prefer to lie down in the night. At such a time the musher must reach down to find out if he has the right stuff.

Over the years, the storms have been vicious, the temperatures unforgiving. There have been animal encounters, sadness, and gladness along the trail. There have been memorable one-time champions and remarkable multiple champions.

For roughly two weeks each February, the Yukon Quest is a self-contained city on the move, mushers and their dogs, race officials and volunteers, and spectators enthralled by a spectacle mixing competition with the harsh elements. Each annual Yukon Quest is an adventure of its own and each musher entered with a dog team lives his own adventure.

This is the story of the history of the Yukon Quest and its storied individuals. It is the story of past champions and past championships, and of how the cast of characters, the mix of characters, entered in the 2009 Quest sought to write new chapters in race lore.

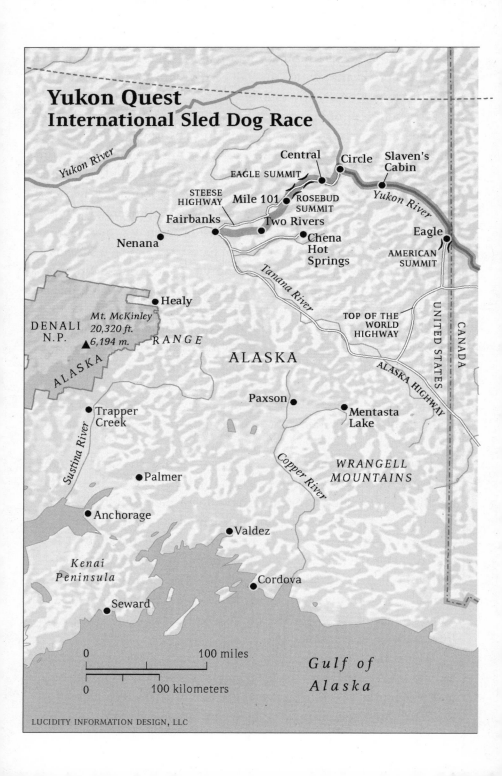

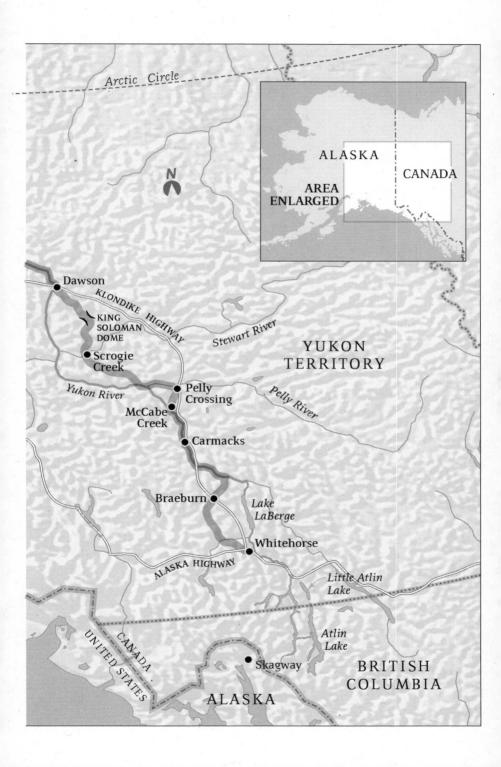

YUKON QUEST ROUTE, WHITEHORSE TO FAIRBANKS*

Distances

CHECKPOINTS & DOG DROP SITES	MILES	KILOMETERS
Whitehorse to Braeburn	100	161
Braeburn to Carmacks	7	11
Carmacks to McCabe Creek	39	63
McCabe Creek to Pelly Crossing	34	55
Pelly Crossing to Stepping Stone	32	51
Stepping Stone to Scroggie Creek	70	113
Scroggie Creek to Dawson City	99	159
Dawson City to 40 Mile River	48	77
40 Mile River to Eagle	99	159
Eagle to Slaven's Roadhouse	101	163
Slaven's Roadhouse to Circle City	58	93
Circle City to Central	74	119
Central to Mile 101	33	53
Mile 101 to Two Rivers	82	132
Two Rivers to Fairbanks	45	72

Note: Distances are approximate because the trail may be rerouted due to weather, terrain, and river conditions in any given year.
*Race runs in opposite direction in even-numbered years.

CHAPTER ONE

MUSHERS ON A QUEST

"Survive first, race second". — Yukon Quest motto

2009 As fall turned into winter, when most of the world was thinking about Christmas and the coming new year of 2009, William Kleedehn visited a friend on the outskirts of Dawson City, a place that at the height of the Klondike Gold Rush more than a century earlier was the liveliest, wildest, and greediest town in the Yukon.

The friend's home was perched on a dome above the frozen city, and Kleedehn knew better than to shut off the engine of his car overnight. He understood that even if he could plug in the engine, the fan belts might shatter like glass when he tried to start it again. The thermometer he left in the vehicle was capable of registering minus 60 Fahrenheit (-51 Celsius), but when Kleedehn glanced at it there was no reading at all. The mercury had sunk below the cutoff point.

"It only gets that cold if you are in the Antarctic," Kleedehn said.

Or, as he had learned, in the Yukon Territory or the Alaskan Interior.

The thermometer showed nothing. The car was parked on a hillside above town. Normally, the cold settles into the valley below, where it is even colder. Ice fog was draped over the town. Kleedehn had driven along the Stewart River on the Klondike Highway from his home south of Whitehorse with a tarp draped over the hood of the car. It didn't help much. The brake pedal and the clutch pedal began to freeze and the steering began to vibrate. His car was freezing to death.

As Kleedehn noted, when your vehicle starts to freeze up while moving, it is damned cold out. Kleedehn did not know if this doesn't-do-it-justice description of "cold snap" was a harbinger of a brutal twenty-sixth annual Yukon Quest International Sled Dog Race, or if the worst of winter would pass prior to the race start on February 14, Valentine's Day 2009, in downtown Whitehorse. But it was something a musher had to prepare for.

As the Quest start approached, forty mushers planned to race for a purse announced at $200,000*. More than a handful of mushers wondered if they had a chance to win.

At age forty-nine, his hair going gray, his face seemingly ruddy from the cold, William Kleedehn planned to make 2009 his final attempt to win the Yukon Quest title after a dozen attempts and two runner-up finishes since 1990. No musher or fan would begrudge him the overdue glory. The phrase "sentimental favorite" was attached to his name with glue. Kleedehn had long before earned the admiration of everyone who followed the race. When he was eighteen, growing up in Germany, Kleedehn lost his left leg below the knee in a motorcycle accident. So Kleedehn had done all of his racing, 12,000 miles (19,312 km) worth of Quest trail, supported by an artificial leg. Without being able to run up hills next to his sled, this meant he couldn't help his dog team in the toughest stretches, as his competitors did. If there was justice in the world, many people thought, Kleedehn deserved to win the Quest just once.

Hans Gatt was one of those people. He said aloud that if he couldn't win the race, he hoped Kleedehn would. Gatt was originally from Elbogen, Austria and gravitated to the open spaces of Alaska and Yukon at first as a sprint musher. When he moved into long-distance racing, Gatt won the Quest three times. Gatt

---

* All currency expressed in U.S. dollars

won the event in 2002, 2003, and 2004, but after skipping the Quest in 2005, he placed second in 2006 and 2007. Hungry to win the Iditarod, he skipped the Quest in 2008.

Gatt, turning fifty by the time of the 2009 race, bred dairy cows and raced motorcycles in Austria. As a young man he decided he wanted to make his living as a professional dog musher. That is akin to an American declaring he wishes to make his fortune in luge racing. "When I announced that I was going to be a professional musher, everybody thought I was crazy," Gatt said.

A fixture in the Far North for two decades, Gatt built a name for himself in Anchorage and Fairbanks, Alaska, with his success in the two- and three-day championship sprint mushing events conducted over 20 and 30 miles (32-48 km) at a time. At the end of the day in sprint racing, dog drivers can sleep in hotels. In 1,000-mile (1,609-km) races, tents are a five-star luxury. Sleep, when it can be grabbed, might be on the floor of a cramped building. Those three-hour naps are blessings breaking up twenty-hour days on the trail while often coping with minus 50 F (-46 C) weather. The average human being on the planet cannot comprehend being outdoors and dealing with the intensity of such temperatures.

"When I tell them it's 40 or 50 below, they have no idea what I'm talking about really," Gatt said.

Like his friend Kleedehn, Gatt was thinking his body had had enough of such challenges. A new lifestyle beckoned. "I'm thinking about retirement," Gatt said in the weeks leading up to the 2009 Quest. "I would definitely spend some time in a warmer climate. The big problem is what to do with the dogs. I'm just not one of those guys who can sell the whole kennel. I love them all."

What everyone knew, but what Gatt would only hint at reluctantly is that before he retired he wanted one more shot at beating Lance Mackey. Mackey was the latest mushing hero. The third member of a championship mushing family to make his mark at the top of the sport was lucky to be alive. A sapping battle with cancer created an unflinching determination in the Fairbanks musher. He had emerged from his brush with death as the best long-distance musher in the world. Mackey had won the Quest a record four straight times and set a speed record between Whitehorse and Fairbanks. Mackey was a one-man, fourteen-dog dynasty. He looked unbeatable and his entry in pursuit of a fifth crown complicated everyone else's aspirations.

Mackey, thirty-eight, had won two straight Iditarod championships. Some years ago it was believed impossible for a musher to finish both the Iditarod and the Quest in the same season. Once that was accomplished it was believed impossible for a musher to do well in both 1,000-mile (1,609-km) races in the same winter. And everyone knew it was impossible for anyone to win both races in the same year. Mackey did the impossible — twice. Entering the 2009 season he had pulled off a double, two years running. Any time Mackey was interviewed, in newspapers, on the radio, on television, or simply met with the public signing autographs (something he found himself doing just about everywhere he went, except to the outhouse), he sang the same tune. "I can't win every race," he said. The problem was that his performance contradicted his words. He did win every race.

It is popular to say that dog mushing is in Mackey's genes. His father, Dick, was one of the organizers of the first Iditarod in 1973 and in 1978 he won the race by one second (the closest finish ever). Lance's half-brother, Rick, is also a past Iditarod and Yukon Quest champion, and his brother Jason entered the 2009 Quest.

Yet, for years, Mackey was more enthralled by commercial fishing than mushing, believing he could make a lot of money netting salmon while he lived in Kasilof on Alaska's Kenai Peninsula. A self-described juvenile delinquent who was more likely to get in trouble and find himself in front of a district court judge than having decisions about his actions ruled on by race judges, Mackey only dabbled in dog breeding and racing until 2001.

Then, almost as soon as Mackey turned serious about mushing, he got sick. A lump in his neck tipped off doctors something was amiss and Mackey endured lengthy, invasive surgery for cancer that in the short run debilitated him and in the long run limited some of his bodily functions. The removal of the lymph glands and saliva glands meant that not the least of Mackey's concerns during a race was an awareness of hydration. Overcoming an illness that might have killed him in order to triumph in the sporting arena has made Mackey a wildly popular and esteemed figure throughout the Far North. The view is that Mackey has met the devil and wrestled him to the ground for a pin and now nothing that happens along the trail, from minus 50 F (-46 C) temperatures to 50 mph (80 kph) winds, can faze him.

"He's tough," said Rick Mackey of Lance. "We always say how our dogs are tougher than the man. I don't know, in Lance's case he might be the tougher one. The cancer changed him. A good friend of the family, who has known Lance since he was born, told Lance. 'Ain't that something? If you hadn't gotten cancer, you wouldn't have done any of this.' There may be a lot of truth in that."

Jon Little, forty-five, was born in England, went to journalism school in Chicago, and worked as a reporter for the *Anchorage Daily News*. When he began mushing, he lived about 75 miles (121 km) from Anchorage, trained dogs in the morning, and worked a night shift at the newspaper. Later, he staffed a news bureau 150 miles (242 km) from the newspaper office. In his hobby time, through patience and hard work, he grew a small kennel of dogs into a team that once placed third in the Iditarod.

No one entering the 2009 Quest faced a more daunting task. Little and his wife, Brie, had two children under the age of three. Recently he had been laid off from his job writing for an outdoors web site. A few months earlier, he had suffered the type of tragedy that preys upon the minds of mushers. Four dogs in his twenty-four-dog kennel were killed during a training run after being hit by a car in the fading light of late evening near his home.

It was late October 2008, just before Halloween. Little was driving one dog team and a friend another, riding on four-wheelers because there was no snow cover yet. At one point, they paused to cross the Sterling Highway, a main thoroughfare on the Kenai

Peninsula. On the way back to the dog yard, it was growing dark. Traffic was heavy. When there was a break, Little waved for the other musher to proceed. However, Little's friend hadn't mounted the four-wheeler, so Little signaled again for him to wait. The musher did not see the second signal.

Coming over the hill was a Subaru Outback traveling 60 mph (97 kph). The driver never saw the team and plowed into the front six dogs. Three huskies died instantly. Another was hurt so badly it had to be put down by a veterinarian. A fifth dog had surgery and was unlikely to compete again. Miraculously, the sixth dog was unharmed.

"It was horrible," a haunted Little said. "They were good dogs."

Little borrowed four dogs from another musher, dogs that were new to him. He called them "front-end" dogs, but they were not as good as the leaders he had lost. Little was very emotional about the death of his dogs, but after flirting with the idea of dropping out, he decided to stay in the race. On top of everything else, he had lost his job that same week.

"I've got enough money to coast on fumes until the Quest is over," Little said. "After that we have some hard decisions to make."

Dog mushing is an expensive sport with the rewards for mushers as much spiritual as aesthetic. With a young family to feed, Little knew that he might be forced to give up long-distance racing for a while if he did not do well. The accident made him more determined than ever to succeed in the 2009 Quest.

Top women finishes are rarities in the Quest. In 1985, when Libby Riddles won the Iditarod, becoming the first female champion, sourdoughs took it personally that a woman could best the rough and tough bearded, long-haired, fur-wearing Alaskan men at such a manly activity. T-shirts appeared overnight announcing "Alaska! Where Men Are Men and Women Win the Iditarod." Susan Butcher followed Riddles, winning four of the next five races and, if Riddles' triumph had been a surprise, Butcher's victories were expected. She had been the next hot musher in line for the crown.

Things were different in the Quest. Fewer women entered and fewer women contended. But in 2000, Alaskan Aliy Zirkle energized the north with a rousing victory. It was a milestone triumph, the first in the race by a woman. Yet Zirkle promptly transferred her attentions to the Iditarod, and the Quest once again suffered from a shortage of top-flight female contenders. That changed in 2008. Michelle Phillips, a Yukoner from Tagish, placed fourth in that year's Quest, injecting her name into pre-race talk about who might win in 2009.

Phillips, forty, and her husband, Ed Hopkins, operate a tourism business giving dog sled rides to visitors. She had shown improvement on the trail. It might be her turn. Phillips, it seemed, was beginning to think along the same lines. "You get to the point where you realize you can be competitive," Phillips said. "You think, 'Okay, if I did that I would have been up there with those front guys.'" Quest fever colored her thoughts.

As an aside to her own aspirations, Phillips carried the hopes of others tucked in her sled. Besides the mandatory gear, from an ax to a sleeping bag, she was transporting one-hundred handcrafted "Feelie Hearts" along the trail to benefit the Hospice Yukon Society. The objects are lopsided fuzzy hearts that are given to comfort the dying and their loved ones. A four-year-old girl who was grieving for her dying mother was given the first one. The story spread and demand grew. The Feelie Hearts riding in Phillips' sled were to sell for $100 each and be accompanied by a copy of her race journal and a photograph of her dog team.

Phillips said the fund-raising was important and personal. The death of loved ones in her own life still affects her, and she wanted to help others cope. "This has helped me acknowledge my grief and work through it," she said.

The least likely musher in the 2009 field, and under no stretch of anyone's imagination a contender, was Newton Marshall, representing the Jamaican Dog Sled Team. Marshall, twenty-five, who had been living and training with Hans Gatt, is from Chuka Cove, Jamaica. It is a place where beach-lovers bask in gentle breezes, not a place where the temperature is measured by the wind chill. For the previous four years, Marshall had given cart rides on the beach and nearby roads to those who wanted to sample the experience of a dog-sled ride without wearing a parka or traveling 5,000 miles (8,047 km) north.

There is a glorious history of the contributions of Siberian huskies, Malamutes, and the current-day Alaska husky mix for transportation in the wilderness, hauling the mail, and for racing excellence. But Marshall's dogs in Jamaica were strays. They were street dogs, animal-pound dogs, and castaways that he picked up and trained to trot.

Sponsors, including renowned singer Jimmy Buffett, a regular visitor to Jamaica, seemingly taken with the whole notion of island mushing, made it possible for Marshall to live and train in the Yukon. Marshall's Jamaican dogs stayed in the warm climate, substituted with northern breeds. While Marshall speaks with a pleasant lilt, there is no mistaking his meaning when he says, "I'm cold."

Marshall was a toddler when another group of Jamaicans made a brief appearance on the world stage of winter sports. The Jamaican bobsled team was an entry in the 1988 Winter Olympics in Calgary and subsequently was the subject of a light-hearted movie called "Cool Runnings." There was great anticipation that Buffet might put in a supportive appearance, perhaps wearing a fur coat over one of his Hawaiian shirts, but Marshall put the kibosh on such speculation. "He says he can't make it," Marshall said with some regret in his voice.

Over the winter in the Yukon, Marshall had experienced the impact of a severe cold spell. This was just months after the latest Jamaican sports hero, Usain Bolt, set world records and won gold medals in sprinting at the Beijing Olympics. Marshall was asked how a victory in the Quest might be measured back home against Bolt's achievements. "Usain Bolt? He has no idea what I'm up against," Marshall said. The real question was whether Marshall did.

One new Quest face was a guy who had seen every type of weather in his mushing career. Technically, he was a rookie because it was his first Quest, but Martin Buser, fifty, four-time Iditarod champion from Big Lake, Alaska, was not a garden-variety newcomer. Originally from Switzerland, Buser took the oath of American citizenship at the Iditarod finish line in Nome in 2002. After twenty-five Iditarod runs, Buser had more long-distance mushing experience than anyone else in the race. Many top Iditarod mushers have done well in the Quest. Vern Halter, Charlie Boulding, Jeff King, Bill Cotter, Rick and Lance Mackey, Ramy Brooks, Joe Runyan, and Lavon Barve are all past Quest champs. There was no reason to think that Buser, with his formidable track record, couldn't be among them.

Buser was the wild card. He owned the Iditarod finish record of 8 days, 22 hours, 46 minutes, a blistering time, and the only finish in less than nine days. He said he always wanted to give the Quest a shot and it finally worked out. His wife, Kathy Chapoton, had retired from teaching and could join him on the trail. His sons, Rohn and Nikolai, named after Iditarod checkpoints, were away at college. "We're empty-nesters," Buser said.

Oh, yeah, and with two boys in college, there were school fees to be paid. Buser said he was going to enter as many races as he could during the winter of 2008-2009. "It's the run for tuition," he said.

For those who understand long-distance mushing, Buser's plan to raise tuition based on the uncertainty of race payoffs sounded as risky as someone jetting off to Las Vegas to raise money to pay the mortgage.

Another contender, a long shot, had inched his way up in the standings in recent years. He was not a favorite, but he kept improving. Sebastian Schnuelle, another transplanted German, with his unbrushable Harpo Marx hair, was a musher to watch. Likewise, Hugh Neff had worked his way up from being a competitor on a shoestring, literally begging for equipment, to being a generous helpmate in the sport. No one counted out Frank Turner, either. Turner was a past champion and Canada's most prominent musher. They all wondered if they could reach the finish line first.

Unlike in other sports, where it is common to find that baseball players don't know about their forebears who worked for slender wages, or football players who are ignorant of predecessors who used inferior equipment and played games in empty stadiums, mushers know their history.

More than any other sporting figures, dog-mushers recognize that they are part of a continuum. They pay homage to those who came before them and appreciate the volunteers who make their events possible.

The men and women of the moment, lining up for the start of the 2009 race, had good memories and long memories. They knew the story of how the Quest came to be.

CHAPTER TWO

A BOLD IDEA

"The route would take Jessie and the rest of the racers over more than 1,000 miles of the most remote, inhospitable region of North America in the heart of the winter, measuring their ability, raw courage, and sheer will with temperatures that often fell between -30 degrees and -50 degrees (F)" — Sue Henry in *Murder on the Yukon Quest*

1983-1984 It was a low-key get-together in April of 1983 in the Bull's Eye Saloon outside of Fairbanks, Alaska. With beer and hamburgers there was discussion of a local sled-dog race that started at the bar and ran to Angel Creek. As the liquor and ideas flowed, someone mentioned that it would be cool if the distance were a little longer than 120 miles (193 km).

LeRoy Shank was at the table, as was Roger Williams. Shank and Williams worked as printers at the *Fairbanks Daily-News Miner*. Shank twice had run the Iditarod. Williams was a history buff who inhaled stories about the gold-rush days and ruminated on them as if they had happened yesterday.

Everyone knew that a trail extended over the hill beyond Angel Creek, and someone said maybe the race should go on to Central, or maybe even to Circle. "Hell, we can go up to the Yukon River and on to Dawson and Whitehorse," Shank recalled saying. "Before the night was over we were going to Rio de Janeiro."

Everyone sobered up soon enough, but the idea lingered. A lot of history connected the region between Fairbanks and Whitehorse — old mail trails, gold prospectors' trails, and trails used by early settlers, trappers, and Natives prior to discovery of gold. Tying together the two cities in a new race made a lot of sense, because of their shared history.

Whitehorse, population 25,000, the capital of Canada's Yukon Territory, lies along the upper Yukon River. It is an important stop for those driving north on the Alaska-Canada Highway. It is the northern rail terminus of the White Pass & Yukon Route, which, combined with the fleet of steam-powered riverboats that served the city, made Whitehorse a key supply center for miners during the gold rush. Like Fairbanks, Whitehorse sees few winters when the temperature doesn't dip to -50 F (-45 C).

Set on the Chena River, Fairbanks was founded in 1901 when a steamboat called the *Lavelle Young* ran aground, and E.T. Barnette established a trading post on the spot. Lucky for him, gold was discovered nearby in 1902, and Fairbanks became a permanent settlement. Today, it is Alaska's second-largest city, some 360 miles (531 km) north of Anchorage. The population of Fairbanks and the surrounding borough is approaching 100,000. Many of Alaska's most successful and best-known mushers live in and around Fairbanks.

No one in their right mind would say the Iditarod was for wimps, but when Shank, Williams, and others plotted the new race, one stretch in the Yukon ran 280 miles (450 km) between checkpoints. By comparision, the longest stretch between checkpoints on the Iditarod is 112 miles (180 km). To face the Yukon Quest challenge, a musher had to be proficient in winter camping skills. Any musher who accepted outside assistance would be disqualified. The message was straightforward: you better be able to take care of yourself.

Why organize a new long-distance race?

"We wanted more of a Bush experience," Shank said, "a race that would put a little woodsmanship into it."

When the Iditarod began, it was more of a long camping trip than race. No one ever had raced a single teams of dogs that far, and no one knew if it could be done. Soon, it became an endurance contest that turned out fresh local sports heroes every March. Yet, as time passed, some purists thought the race had become tilted towards wealthier mushers with large kennels who hop-scotched to villages every 50 miles (80 km). People like Shank and his friends wondered if the Iditarod had strayed too far from its origins. Eventually their wild ideas conceived in a bar became a goal as they set out to create an alternative for the poor man's musher — a race that could be entered without courting bankruptcy and that demanded more self-sufficiency on the trail.

Like those who conceived the Iditarod race, no one was certain this new event, temporarily called "The Fairbanks to Whitehorse Race" — but sorely in need of a sexier name — could be jump-started organizationally, let alone be completed by mushers.

Shank and Williams became the co-founders. They hustled for money and volunteers, committee workers, and planners. They also had to tip-toe around approaching the proper people in the Yukon because the race crossed an international boundary. The United States and Canada may be the closest of allies, may have the longest undefended border in the world, but the more the Alaskans talked, the more they realized how different the two nations were — two peoples separated by a common language.

"We were having trouble crossing international borders, municipal property, tribal property, federal property, and provincial property," Williams said. "You're dealing really with two different cultures. I think we paved the way for some good Canadian-American relations. In those days, nothing happened in the Yukon without the government."

Somehow the twain met. Shank said Williams could have been a terrific lawyer.

On August 27, 1983, the first announcement of the race appeared in the *Daily News-Miner*. The news story was written by sports editor Bob Eley, who reported, "It's still in the infant stages, but if everything goes according to plan, there will be a second 1,000-mile sled-dog race in Alaska next March, along with the Iditarod."

The story was life-altering for Eley. Although he is still the *News-Miner* sports editor, Eley left the newspaper for a time to serve as executive director of the race in the 1980s. He served more than one term as president of the board of directors and still volunteers his time to manage the Fairbanks dog-mushing museum.

Eley was smitten from the start, believing the creation of the race was good for the town. "I wouldn't say it's why people stay here, but it makes you look forward with something to do in winter," Eley said. "When it is 45 degrees (F) below zero and you can't see past your nose in ice fog, you know there's something cool going to happen here in a few weeks," he said, "and it's not just for Fairbanks now. I think its slowly gained popularity throughout the state. When it first got started it was pretty much the Fairbanks area. Now it's gone international. There are always film crews from around the world."

At first, the word "international" referred only to the customs house at the border between Alaska and Beaver Creek in the Yukon where mushers' trucks crossed. Media visits from Germany, France, England, and Japan are regular occurrences now, not something easily foreseen in the beginning.

Shank, Williams, and other organizers followed up the *News-Miner* article with a public meeting to determine the level of musher interest. The first meeting attracted seven people. The organizers believed that Fairbanks would adopt the race as its own, but they knew they had to sell the idea.

They had been talking about the race for weeks, hoping to raise a $50,000 purse, but did not yet have any competitors. Thirty-eight people turned out at a second meeting. At a third meeting in the fall, a Fairbanks musher named Murray Clayton presented organizers with a $500 entry fee. Clayton became the first musher to enter the Fairbanks-to-Whitehorse race. Being cautious, Shank and Williams suggested it might be best to wait another year, until February 1985, to run the first race. But Clayton's act provided momentum. The heck with waiting a year, it was decided, they were going to birth this baby in less than six months.

When Joe Redington set out to establish the Iditarod in an era when the only sled dog racing was sprint races with a maximum one-day distance of 30 miles (48 km), he was still seeking to raise funds for the promised purse even after the dog drivers had hit the trail. Shank and his group had no such difficulty raising the $50,000 payoff.

"We had it by Christmas," Shank said.

Eventually, the race acquired a flashy name too. With help from his wife, Kathleen, Shank tossed out several ideas and he and others mulled over all suggestions. A contest was conducted. Nominees included "The Northern Iditarod" and "The Gold Rush 1,000-Mile Race." Shank wanted the race to shout "Yukon!" — "the Yukon Something."

One day, Shank and Wendy Waters, who had founded the 200-mile (322-km) Percy de Wolfe race in Canada, flipped through the *World Book Dictionary* and stumbled upon the word "quest." Shank liked that—a "quest." A more romantic name replaced the here-to-there working title. It became The Yukon Quest International Sled Dog Race. To this day, Shank keeps the dictionary in the kitchen of his Two Rivers, Alaska home. The word "quest" is highlighted in yellow.

The brainstorm at the bar evolved into a new long-distance race with a brand new name, a solid purse, and a trail to follow. It was decided that the finish line would alternate each year between Fairbanks and Whitehorse. The first race started in Alaska, passing through tiny communities and over mountain passes that would gain fame during the ensuing years. Mushers traveled through settlements rich with gold-rush history — Central, Circle City, and Eagle in Alaska, and Dawson City, Pelly Crossing, Carmacks, and Braeburn in the Yukon, following the frozen Yukon River much of the way. They climbed over 4,002-foot (1,200-meter) King Solomon's Dome, American Summit, and the greatly feared Eagle Summit. In the early years, the race traversed Lake Laberge, legendary during gold-rush days.

Time has brought adjustments to the course. If you want to hear about Lake Laberge, you will have to read Jack London, not the *Whitehorse Star* race reports. The race bypasses the lake now. The race founders wanted the Quest to be difficult, and it was. A lonely 280 miles (450 km) stretched between Dawson City, the halfway point, and the first Alaska checkpoint of Circle City — the longest distance between checkpoints. Mushers would have to camp along the way.

John Firth, a Yukoner who has written a book about the Quest and served as president of the event's Canadian board, called the race "the last great adventure."

A GRAND ADVENTURE it has been. From the start, Jeff King guessed the Quest would be something special.

King lives in a remote cabin a few miles removed from the Parks Highway in Interior Alaska. His address is Denali Park where one of North America's most famous national parks is located. In the summer of 1983, he was a young musher, just breaking into long-distance races, far less experienced than the savvy, four-time Iditarod champion he is now.

His post office received mail delivery just twice a week and outside stood a *News-Miner* newspaper coin box. One day, a headline arrested his attention. It was above Bob Eley's story about the new race. King had raced in the 1981 Iditarod, his debut, but didn't have the money to return. He figured that he could handle the new race's lesser costs.

"I was pathetically broke," King recalled, and felt he was way behind the best mushers in experience. No one would have more experience than anyone else in a new race. "That was a real motivator. I would have as good a chance as anybody."

The freshness of the event excited King. For those who missed out on the start of the Iditarod, it was like a second chance to be a pioneer. "Are we even going to be able to make it? What are we going to run into? Those were some of the questions mushers pondered aloud.

Bill Cotter of Nenana, Alaska, was the checker at the first checkpoint on the first Iditarod. At the time, he was focused on sprint mushing, but soon crossed over to distance racing. He had missed out on traveling the trail in the first Iditarod and he was determined to race in the first Quest. Like King, he thought it was a second opportunity to be a pioneer.

Sonny Lindner of Two Rivers, Alaska, also was drawn to the Quest by the original newspaper story. "I thought it sounded like fun," Lindner said. "I thought it would be interesting to cross new country and it sounded as if it might be only a one-time thing."

The blond Lindner, who resembles Robert Redford, is pals with his neighbor, Rick Swenson, at the time a four-time Iditarod champion and now the only five-time winner. They shot the breeze about the race and wondered about rules that differed from the Iditarod. Quest mushers had to carry a minimum of fifty pounds of dog food in their sled. That meant they were going to be transporting more weight.

Lindner, then thirty-four, had considerable experience with rural freighting, traveling from one remote spot to another carrying heavy loads in his sled. He liked the idea that there were long distances in the Quest with nobody around. Winter camping and relying on outdoor skills appealed to him. Swenson urged him to go for it and lent Lindner his prize leader, Andy, still one of the most esteemed lead dogs in Iditarod history.

On the other side of the border, Frank Turner was as excited as anyone when he heard about the Yukon Quest. Turner had grown up in Toronto and earned a social-work degree in college. In 1973, he and a friend agreed on a flip of the coin to choose a vacation spot. Turner wanted to go to Mexico, his friend to Whitehorse. Turner lost the coin flip. They traveled to Whitehorse, went fishing and hiking, had fun, but Turner had no plans to stay or return. As a souvenir of the North he bought a puppy and named it Skookum.

Turner did not know what he wanted to do with the rest of his life, but when the car reached Ontario and he was surrounded again by houses and stores and traffic he realized he no longer wanted to live there. "It was a spontaneous reaction to the big chimneys and piles of rock and stuff," Turner recalled. "From that moment on I knew that I was just waiting to go back to the Yukon. It was kind of like an epiphany for me."

Living in the Yukon, Turner expanded his dog ownership to a full team. He raced middle-distance events and jumped at the chance to do a marathon race when the Quest was created.

THE FIRST Yukon Quest started in Fairbanks on February 25, 1984. There were twenty-six entries, not a deep field, but based on future accomplishments, one filled with luminaries. Seven racers who entered eventually would win at least one Quest or Iditarod race.

The rules limited racers to twelve dogs, fewer than the fourteen allowed now. It was unclear how smooth the trail would be, so many mushers took precautions to protect their sleds. Lindner had extra thick runners. It seemed unlikely anyone was going to run away with the title, but Lindner and Joe Runyan, a future champ, made the first push for the lead, controlling the early pace to Eagle. Cotter, King, and Iditarod veteran Harry Sutherland closed the gap as the temperature dropped to minus 50 F (-45 C). The chill immediately established one of the traits of the Quest — it was going to be a cold, cold race.

The trail was no smooth highway. A trail was put in two weeks before the race started and that meant two weeks of winter weather had pounded it before the first musher headed out. "They had the philosophy they weren't going to touch it again until after the race, or something like that," Cotter said. "So we did a lot of trail-breaking and we had a lot of portages on the river. It was plenty tough. We took turns holding teams and cutting brush with our axes. It was very cold. All I remember about the Quest is fifty below. It was fun that first year, though."

The mushers were told Canadians were going to meet them to escort them across the border at an area called the Thousand Islands, but when the competitors reached the spot they saw no one. They could barely see anything through falling snow and saw no broken trail, so they waited through the night. Daylight brought no assistance, so the mushers teamed up, counting on their best leaders to find the trail.

"It was dangerous as hell," Runyan said. "There was open water and glare ice. We just worked our way through that area, but if we hadn't had those good leaders there was no way in hell we could have gone through there. I had good trap-line leaders who were used to that stuff."

King was impressed with Lindner's leaders, Andy, and a lesser dog called Lizard. He was even more impressed with Lindner's trail chow. Other mushers chomped on granola bars, sandwiches, and the like, while Lindner's grub appeared to be catered by a four-star restaurant. Lindner cooked a steak and carried an omelet pan. King stared and "just marveled at his ingenuity." Whether trying to do so or not, Lindner psyched out the competition with his menu.

Lindner laughed at the memory. At the time a meat company was one of his sponsors. Knowing roadhouses and food-buying opportunities were going to be intermittent, Lindner made sure he was flush with mouth-watering goodies. Forget trail mix. "I had surf and turf," Lindner said, "steak and lobster tail. When I fired up the dog cooker I always had an omelet pan with butter going." Lindner was not always so fortunate in long-distance races. In his first Iditarod, a hunting friend loaded him down with goat stew. Lindner's trail specialties never got fancier than they were in the first Quest.

The front-runners needed one another for a while as they felt out the trail, but as the group moved closer to Whitehorse it was apparent that Lindner had the fastest team. He didn't even need Andy in lead, leaving him in wheel position in case he needed the aging dog's power late in the race.

"Sonny had by far the strongest team," Cotter said.

That was apparent by Maisy May on the Stewart River. Most of the mushers let Lindner go. He figured they wanted him to break trail and burn out. By Stepping Stone, still shy of Pelly Crossing and the Klondike Highway, only Sutherland remained with Lindner and Lindner started to put distance on the Alaskan's team a few hundred miles from Whitehorse. Lindner took a four-hour break and no one caught up to him. However, sitting at a camp in the fog, he thought he was lost.

"There were no trail markers," Lindner said. "It looked like the main trail and the best way to go. I was worried, so I turned around, went back for a while, and ran into Harry. When I said something about maybe being lost, he said, "'Are you kidding? We're following your trail.' I turned around again and took off back the other way. I had to go through Stepping Stone again, but I kept a couple of hours ahead of Harry. That's when I thought I could keep up that pace."

He could. No one caught him because they had the same difficulties with the trail and visibility.

Lindner had brought the right dogs and the right mindset to the Quest. He planned for it to be long, cold, and on difficult terrain and he chose tough dogs to cope with that scenario. When the situation played out as planned, he was ready.

Lindner reached Whitehorse 12 days and 5 minutes after leaving Fairbanks and won $15,000. Sutherland was second, more than five hours behind him, followed by Cotter, Runyan, and King. Turner finished fourteenth in his first Quest. He had not fared particularly well, but he was hooked.

Shank was happier to see Lindner arrive in Whitehorse than if he had discovered a new gold rush. As Lindner approached the downtown business district, Shank exulted. "It was a relief when Sonny Lindner crossed the finish line in Whitehorse," he said. "That made the Quest real, because if one guy did it, it could be done. Some of the guys had come up to me and said, 'Oh, you'll never make it.' Well, we did make it."

Despite Lindner's worry that he might be running the first and only Quest, the race thrived. More than a quarter of a century later, a Quest championship is one of the top prizes in dog-mushing and Sonny Lindner has victory No. 1 on his resume.

CHAPTER THREE

A MAN WITH A DREAM

"This is the law of the Yukon,
and ever she makes it plain:
'Send not your foolish and feeble;
send me your strong and your sane.'"
—Poet Robert Service, *The Law of the Yukon*

2009 Hugh Neff grew up in the Chicago area where dogs were pets and his only connection to sled-dog racing was reading books about the Iditarod or stories penned by Jack London. In 1995, by the time he was in his twenties, these tales of the frigid frontier had kindled the spark of northern romance and overwhelmed his soul.

He hitch-hiked to Alaska and began life as the low man on the totem pole in a dog yard. Dog-handlers make less money than waitresses, generally being paid in room and board and knowledge.

In 2000, after furthering his mushing education, Neff, by then thirty-three, entered the Yukon Quest. Using borrowed dogs or those gathered from a pound, and with a race budget so low at $200 he had to borrow shoestrings never mind live on one, Neff headed out on the trail. His supplies were so limited the raggedy Neff appalled veteran mushers with his ignorance and need to beg food when he ran short. Somehow, he finished thirteenth and won $2,100.

That was the shaky beginning. Neff built his confidence and his kennel, got smarter and faster. In 2001, he was the Iditarod's rookie of the year. Each year, despite living poor, Neff raced the Yukon Quest and Iditarod, putting more miles on his odometer and putting a bit more luster on his reputation.

When he was twelve, Neff delivered newspapers and worked as a golf-club caddy to make money. It was not difficult for him to live a fairly Spartan existence in the North, especially when his girlfriend, Tamra Reynolds, helped out. When Neff won the Quest's halfway prize of four ounces of gold in Dawson City, he pledged to melt it down into a wedding ring for Reynolds. But the transformation was slow to occur.

"It's still sitting in my dresser drawer," Neff said of the gold before the 2009 race. Tamra retorted that Neff was going to make it happen "when he wins a race."

It was well known that Neff's lifestyle simulated a vow of poverty, so when he rose at the Quest's breakup banquet at the end of the 2008 race and pledged to pay newcomer Josh Cadzow's 2009 entry fee of $1,500, people were startled. Cadzow, just twenty, an Alaska Native from Fort Yukon, Alaska,had dominated a 300-mile (483-km) qualifying race. He barely knew Neff, and he wasn't even in the room. "I was really stunned," said Cadzow, whose uncle Jay is a former racer.

Neff's largesse stemmed from an inheritance. His father died and it turned out he had a stash of cash that no one knew about. "I just need dog food, some macaroni and cheese and hot dogs," Neff said. Neff preferred helping others to buying trophy automobiles or yachts. "Your dogs are your real trophies," he said.

There was only one trophy he truly coveted — one symbolizing first place. Neff had finished ninth in 2007 and seventh in 2008. Few mentioned his name as a top contender for 2009. What looked to be the toughest and deepest field ever in a Quest, in December and January suffered casualties steadily leading up to departure day. One by one many serious contenders and beginners pulled out. Bad weather prevented some racers from completing their middle-distance qualifying races. Injuries slowed others. And financial considerations affected still more. It all proved that just getting out of the starting gate could be a challenge in the Quest.

Frank Turner, who sat out only one of the first twenty-five Quests, scratched. He had a separated shoulder, suffered on a training run, and was signing up for surgery instead of the race. Four-time defending champ Lance Mackey made the agonizing choice to skip the Quest. He had been offered $50,000 – more than the first-place $30,000 prize, by the Alaska Army National Guard, to train a Native musher named Harry Alexie from Kwethluk, Alaska and supply him with dogs. Mackey said he didn't have enough top-notch dogs in training to do everything.

Even worse for the remaining mushers was a shortfall in the purse. Expected to be $200,000, the race organizers hustled to guarantee a $150,000 payoff, though they hadn't stopped fund-raising. The worldwide economic crisis didn't help. The stock market plummeted in the United States. Unemployment increased. Sponsorship money in Alaska and Canada dried up. The economic landscape was as harsh as the terrain along the trail.

Officials hoped this reality was a temporary blip in what had been steady growth of popularity in the Quest. There had been crises before of one nature or another, but they always had been resolved. Some were financial. Some were based on friction between the boards of directors on each side of the international boundary. Once, the Canadian board resigned en masse. At other times, the dual authorities dueled over money and policy. In recent years, peace had reigned, but there were often little conflicts brewing, borne of having more than one set of leaders. Both sides accommodated themselves to reality and somehow made it all work without detriment to the long-term health of the race.

STEPHEN REYNOLDS, originally from the Toronto area, moved to Whitehorse on a three-month conservation project contract and stayed. The 2009 race marked his seventh (and what turned out to be last) race as executive director for Yukon Quest Canada. He took over in 2002 when the old board's frustration over financial difficulties peaked.

"The Yukon Quest in the Yukon was desperately close to its dying breath," Reynolds said.

No more. Reynolds said that the appreciation and attitude among residents was always there, but better connections had to be made in the business community. "Within the Yukon Territory," he said, "the Yukon Quest is the big event. We are easily the single largest winter event that occurs in the Yukon Territory and in terms of awareness globally and in terms of economic impact."

The ripple effect of cash spent in the Yukon during the Quest is $1.5 million, Reynolds said, and more people visit from far corners of the earth each year. Just three years earlier, the purse was $125,000 and while $200,000 was promised for 2009, the economy was hindering efforts to raise it. "Businesses and corporations are extremely cautious with their investments and their community giving at this point in time," he said. "We were just in the market as the economic collapse began."

Still, what pleased Reynolds was that the relationship between Canadian and Alaskan race leaders had been cemented. Old-timers told him stories about meetings breaking up with "fists clenched and their teeth grinding." The political divisions made people ill, but they seem to have dissipated.

Perhaps that's because the executive director of Yukon Quest Alaska was a Canadian, too. Tania Simpson is from Vancouver "I fell in love with it," Simpson said of the race.

The Quest is seductive. Racers put up with some of the most extreme conditions on the planet and as soon as they get home they forget they were even chilly. And every year new faces turn up seeking to conquer the race that boasts severe cold, howling winds, and rugged landscape, even if, like Neff, they can't really afford it.

Long-time trapper Wayne Hall from Eagle, Alaska, one of the tiny communities that serve as a checkpoint on the trail, races periodically, when he can muster the entry fee. "The Quest wouldn't exist without sponsors," he said. "Mushers wouldn't race unless they were independently wealthy, which most of us are not."

Rookie Mark Sleightholme, thirty, from Mossley, England didn't sound as if he would have much money left in the bank after his Quest run. "Thank God for Visa," he said. Sleightholme listed his Visa card as his only sponsor in his official race biography.

One of the most eye-catching financial plans among long-distance mushers is the ongoing fund-raiser for Dave Dalton, fifty-one, of Healy, Alaska, a one-time taxi-cab driver in Fairbanks who used to drive strippers home after their late-night shifts at the Reflections night club. Dalton is a long-time friend of the owner. The strippers come on stage attired in Dalton mushing T-shirts, then peel them off and offer them for auction. What ordinarily sells for $15 to the general public suddenly gains value after covering luscious flesh. "The guys bid on them and they go for $75, or even $150," Dalton said. The proceeds help purchase dog food.

Quest officials stuck to more traditional fund-raising, hoping to increase the purse as mushers headed out on the trail.

Valentine's Day was quite sunny, though the temperature in downtown Whitehorse was -32 F degrees (-36 C). Tim Horton's doughnut shop did a booming hot-coffee business. Parked a few blocks away from the start, their trucks purring in the cold air, inexperienced mushers hastily organized gear, and veterans calmly assessed their sled belongings.

The eyelashes of Jamaican Newton Marshall were frosted, providing his face with an other-worldly look. "I'm really nervous," he said.

When the mushers drew start positions at a kickoff banquet two nights before, Kyla Boiven wore a slinky black dress accented by long, glittery earrings and a necklace. She got wolf whistles. Then she read a poem expressing her feelings about heading out on the trail for a sixth time. "Tonight I'm lost in dog dreams," she said, "...and tomorrow the long run begins."

Some knew what to expect from past runs. Others only knew the Quest by reputation. Colleen Robertia, thirty-two, an elementary school teacher of disturbed children, was a rookie from Kasilof, Alaska, counting on husband Joseph as chief handler. Anticipating competitive tension, she said she hoped they were still married by race's end. Robertia frantically prepared, making sure she had the necessary trail items. "I haven't slept in three weeks," she said.

It wasn't as if she was going to catch up anytime soon.The Yukon Quest is a sleep- deprivation event where mushers cat-nap for a couple of hours at a time and try to stay upright while their sleds bump along the trail.

Before he marched his dogs to the starting line wearing cute white Northern Outfitter coats, Martin Buser hugged his wife, Kathy Chapoton. For Valentine's Day, she gave him a Lindt chocolate bar, Swiss, of course.

"It's his favorite," she said.

The breakfast of champions.

Sebastian Schnuelle, thirty-eight, of Whitehorse, but originally from Germany, generally has a playful, teasing attitude. He is easy-going and even as a serious racer this shows through. One of his dogs is named "Herring," because it is so skinny, Schnuelle said. While some mushers say they love being in a race with checkpoints 200 miles (321 km) apart, Schnuelle said the more checkpoints the merrier. "I think I'm a sissy because I like checkpoints."

Schnuelle is easily identifiable by his wild and unruly hair. If he played football, Schnuelle would have difficulty squeezing his hair into a helmet. Instead of a hard-shell hat, however, on race morning Schnuelle pulled on a gray, children's dog's head hat that occasioned much comment. It was little more than a toy.

Schnuelle put up with the chill to entertain fans, but switched head covering just around the corner. For sure, the cold was just around the corner, ahead in the tunnel of spruce trees, on the frozen Yukon River, and in surrounding hills and mountains.

Thomas Tetz, another German transplant to the Yukon, and a Quest veteran, recently backed away from the race to enjoy other outdoor pursuits. He was part of a mountaineering team that climbed Mount Logan, at 19,551 feet (5,959 meters), the tallest mountain in Canada. Tetz paused when asked which is colder, racing the Yukon Quest or climbing Logan. "They're about the same," Tetz said. "But on the Quest, when you are cold, you can get to a cabin. On Logan, there is only the tent."

Cold comfort for the mushers.

Neff, starting his seventh Quest, was laid-back. He was no longer the edgy beginner. He could laugh at his younger self, how he had acted before making his Quest debut. "The week before the race I borrowed two dogs," he said. "I was putting my sled together the night before the race. Sometimes you've got to take risks in life."

In one way or another, all twenty-eight mushers heading into the wilderness of the Yukon were taking risks. Nobody knew what the race would bring.

CHAPTER FOUR

THE RACE TAKES HOLD

"When a man journeys into a far country he must be prepared to forget many of the things he has learned and to acquire such customs as are inherent with existence in the new land." — Jack London, *In a Far Country*

1985-1988 When the Yukon Quest was conceived, Joe Runyan was making his living trapping marten in Alaska, running a team of the typical huskies of the time, each weighing more than sixty pounds (27 kilos). His trap lines covered a vast territory and that gave his dogs seasoning. Standing tall and slender, Runyan often wore a goofy-looking hat reminiscent of an old-time pilot's hat with flaps that covered his ears. He spoke slowly, but thoughtfully, and had a sly wit. He was trail-savvy and he thought he was equipped properly with a solid sled for the Quest's often lumpy trail.

The dogs were pullers, not speedsters, but he still finished fourth in the inaugural Quest.

"It's more of an adventure race," Runyan said, explaining why the event appealed to him. "I figured I had good dogs and that, after the first year, I could get better."

He did.

Race newcomer Rick Atkinson of Scotland by way of Bettles, Alaska, set the early pace in 1985 and was hours ahead arriving in Dawson. Atkinson had been a mountaineering guide and mushed dogs in Antarctica, so he was no cold-weather novice. He was not, however, an experienced racer. Runyan stopped on the outskirts of the historic gold-rush town to help an old man whose truck was stuck, and that let Atkinson get away, but he was confident he could catch him on the clear and packed Yukon stretch of trail.

Several of the same guys from the year before were also in the hunt, including Harry Sutherland, Jeff King, and Bill Cotter. But Sonny Lindner had not returned to defend his title. Two nights out of Dawson, Runyan saw a light in the distance. He was sure it was Atkinson. Gradually, Runyan reeled him in. When he passed Atkinson, Runyan felt he had control of the race.

At Chena Hot Springs, the optimistic Runyan was only about 60 miles (97 km) from the finish line in Fairbanks. After being assured that the trail had been smoothed, Runyan discovered a maze of confusing, unmarked trails. He later was told that the person responsible for breaking the trail chose to spend his time at a bar.

"If you don't have markings and you don't know that country, it's hopeless," Runyan said. "I had to ask people where the hell the trail was to Fairbanks. You don't want to blow it in the last fifty miles. Word got out and some people put some flagging in."

While Runyan frantically attempted to find his way to the finish, Atkinson closed the gap. After all, he only had to follow Runyan. "I figured everybody was going to catch me because I was screwing around not sure where to go," Runyan said. But Atkinson never caught him.

Runyan mushed into Fairbanks on the frozen Chena River with eleven dogs late at night. The finish line was crowded with so many fans there was a momentary fear that they might break through the ice. Nerves shot, Runyan felt as much relief as joy when he was crowned champion of the second Yukon Quest. His winning time was just twenty minutes faster than Atkinson's and he was ninety minutes ahead of Sutherland. It was the first major championship of Runyan's mushing career.

Most important to organizers, the completion of the 1985 Quest was proof that the race was here to stay. The Quest was no fluke.

Something else was apparent. Leading finishers wanted another crack at the title. In the mid to late 1980s, they kept coming back.

They had picked up trail knowledge and wanted to use it. There were thirty-nine entries in the 1986 race, fifteen of them returnees.

After a year off, Lindner returned to the field in crisp minus 30 F (-1 C) temperatures and took the early lead on the Fairbanks side. Not far back were King, Cotter, and Joe May, the 1980 Iditarod champion. Running at the front was Tim Osmar, then nineteen, a commercial fisherman from Clam Gulch, Alaska, and the son of the 1984 Iditarod winner, Dean Osmar. Moving up was Bruce Johnson from Atlantic River, British Columbia. Johnson had finished sixth in the first Quest and eighth in the second. Mushers fought their way through deep snow, but May was the first into Dawson for the mandatory thirty-six-hour rest stop. Lindner was not far behind him in second, and Johnson followed in third. The snowy conditions slowed the pace and kept the mushers clustered together, battling the elements more than each other.

For four days, the sticky flakes fell, wiping out the trail and making it difficult for sleds to move smoothly. Granular and sticky, the snow balled up in dogs' feet where the snow cover was thinnest and the animals had to break trail where the snow came up to their chests. No racer wanted to risk burning out his team by breaking the entire trail alone, so they stuck together. Leaving Carmacks, 100 miles (161 km) from Whitehorse, the contenders acknowledged that the conditions would decide the winner. The last man to break trail, Sutherland said, might well be the champ.

The weather never improved. Near the end, eight inches of new snow fell, and fog disrupted visibility. An estimated 2,000 fans waited at the finish line in Whitehorse to greet the winner of the $15,000 first prize. The wild stretch run seemed more like Churchill Downs at the end of the Kentucky Derby than a sled dog race, the top seven places finishing within ninety-five minutes of one another. The champ was Johnson, beating King by twenty-four minutes.

Illustrating just how the deluge of snow had affected the race, Johnson's winning time of more than fourteen days was three days slower than Runyan's finish the year before. Johnson said the turning point was on Lake Laberge. "I started out in a total whiteout," he said. "I couldn't see, but I knew my dogs could take it. We took the lead and held it. I called it the Lake Laberge charge."

Johnson was a popular winner. But the best mushers who had been present at the creation also believed they could one day become champs, and they kept at it.

It meant something special to Bill Cotter to be part of the first Yukon Quest. The Nenana musher was involved in sprint mushing during the glory days of the Anchorage Fur Rendezvous, had been a volunteer on the first Iditarod, and had entered the Iditarod when he could afford to take time off from his job as an electrician. Being part of the 1984 Quest, when it promised adventure on a little-known trail, excited him. He placed third that year, fifth in 1985, and sixth in 1986. In 1987, he wanted to make the Quest his own.

"After the first year, I felt that I could win the thing, so I kept trying," Cotter said.

The wilder the wilderness, the happier Cotter is mushing dogs, but he enjoyed the social aspect of the race best — the camping with fellow mushers, telling stories around a fire, stopping at checkpoints, and the teamwork it sometimes took to get through the adventure. He and Lindner broke most of the trail during the heavy snows of the previous year — more than their share, he believed. When other teams passed and finished ahead of them, Cotter was peeved. "I just had this fire in my stomach that said I was going to win the next year."

Cotter raced hard in 1987. He was the first among the thirty-nine mushers into Carmacks from Whitehorse and believed he had fended off all challengers by the time he reached the outskirts of Fairbanks. It was a year when the temperatures were brutal, dropping to minus 60 F (15 C) at one point. He had a three-hour lead on Dave Monson a day from the finish, and put his dogs on cruise control. Monson, who had attended law school in South Dakota with another musher, Vern Halter, eventually would write his own Quest history and marry four-time Iditarod champion Susan Butcher.

Like most mushers, Monson tried to think of ways to stay fresh on the trail, whether sleeping standing up on the sled runners, as many racers did or by other means. "There's no compromise for good dental hygiene," Monson said in a conversation with musher Martin Buser. Buser agreed: "It wakes you up. It's like a half-hour nap."

It's not clear if Monson brushed his teeth in Two Rivers on the charge to the finish, but he definitely woke Cotter up. Rather than basking in the glow of victory before it was official, Cotter remembered what baseball great Yogi Berra had said: "It's never over 'til it's over."

About five miles (eight kilometers) from the finish line, a helicopter flew overhead. Cotter knew it carried a camera crew from a TV station following the race. He waved as the chopper hovered over the trail behind him. "Whoa," he thought, "there's a team behind me!" It was Monson, clipping along, shaving the lead.

Cotter started pumping his foot alongside the sled. Monson chased him all the way to Fairbanks and finished second ten minutes behind. Cotter reflected on the closeness of the finish. "It's like a hundredth of a second in swimming," he said.

No one served cake for Cotter at the finish, who celebrated his forty-first birthday on the trail, but he was as pleased as he ever was following a race. "It's an incredible feeling of accomplishment," he said. "I was ecstatic with the way the dogs performed. I was really, really happy."

For good reason. Like "senator" or "judge", "Yukon Quest champion" is a life-long title.

Cotter spent most of the next twenty years focused on the Iditarod, placing as high as third. Every once in a while, as he approached and then passed his sixtieth birthday, he announced his retirement from mushing, sometimes in forums as public as the podium at an Iditarod breakup banquet in Nome. Now he makes fun of himself. "I've retired more times than Michael Jordan," Cotter said.

In 2006, Cotter had a good reason to retire: he suffered a stroke that afflicted his left side. It affected his walking, the strength in his left arm, and speech. Cotter attacked rehab with more determination than he had any race. "It was a battle," he said. "I learned how to walk again. Sometimes, when I get tired, I limp a little bit on the left side. I'm not as strong as I was before, but my coordination is back."

Cotter sold most of his racing dogs, but after getting back into shape he acquired some puppies and for amusement started training them. In 2008, to prove he was still the Bill Cotter of old, he again entered the Quest. Never did fourteenth place feel so good.

And Monson? A year after the pursuit of Cotter, he beat a field of forty-seven mushers to Whitehorse and collected a $20,000 purse for first place. Monson was ahead at the halfway point in Dawson and won handily, nine hours ahead of Alaskan Gerald Riley, a past Iditarod champion.

Of all the ways exhaustion could manifest itself at the end of a long race, Monson's feet gave him the most trouble. When Monson talked about barking dogs, he wasn't referring to his huskies. At the finish line, he not only undid his boots, but also peeled off socks and other layers. He stood barefoot in the snow talking about his journey.

"My feet are killing me," he said. "I just know that if I had to go much farther, my feet would have given out."

If he hadn't hustled indoors quickly, Monson might have become the first Quest musher to suffer frostbite after the race was over instead of during it.

CHAPTER FIVE

THE COMEBACK

"An old-timer cares for his dogs, then himself." — Jack London, *To the Man on Trail*

1989 Jeff King was a crazy man. His doctors told him so. There was no way he could race in the Yukon Quest in 1988, not without risking frostbite or more damage to an already-wounded hand. Stay home this time, Jeff, the doc said. But no, King entered the first Quest in 1984 and he wanted to keep his record going of appearing in every one of the races between Fairbanks and Whitehorse.

The Quest is a sled-dog race and it is the dogs that get pampering along the trail, not the humans. The dogs' blankets are warmer, their straw is thicker. Their food is richer in protein as they devour 10,000 calories of eats per day. The dogs are fed and set up in camp to rest before the human takes a break. That is the rule of the land and anyone who breaks it is foolish at best and likely to be disqualified at worst.

The Yukon Quest is densely populated by veterinarians who examine paws and shoulders, take weights and measurements at regular intervals along the trail. The mushers? They are on their own, perhaps able to beg an aspirin here or there. But they have signed up for discomfort and they expect it, whether it is aching muscles, lack of sleep shivering bodies, or bruises from sleds bashing trees or bouncing over trail potholes.

All of that stuff happens along the trail. Worse is the case of a musher ailing before he heads out onto the trail. In 1988, King should not have left the starting line.

The preceding August, King was working in wood on his Denali Park homestead when he slashed his left wrist and hand with a skill-saw blade. "I cut everything important in my left wrist," he said.

To know Jeff King is to recognize that he is one of the most competitive men in the galaxy. He is of medium height and weighs roughly 140 pounds (63 kilos). When he's dieting he is as single-minded as a beauty pageant contestant. He was a high-school wrestler and football player and is someone who hungers to win at everything from Monopoly to mushing. Including his numerous victories in middle-distance races, as well as his four Iditarod titles, King is possibly the most successful sled-dog racer of all time. So, as long as his cut healed and he could bandage it sufficiently to protect it, he believed he could race. Medical opinions suggested otherwise. In a race where the temperature was likely to plunge to minus 50 F (10 C), King's lack of feeling in the left hand could be a dangerous handicap. The cold could destroy his flesh without him being aware of it.

"The doctor said, 'It's not a matter of if, it's a matter of when,' " King recalled. "And I just went, 'Bullshit, I can do this.' "

King worked with a sponsor to design a special mitten. Not only was it going to be extra warm, it also would accommodate a meat thermometer inserted into the cloth with a sensor. King could read the temperature without taking off the mitten.

"I was going to outsmart this thing," he said.

Instead, the cold out-smarted him. Leaving Fairbanks, the temperature was minus 35 F (-1 C) degrees and the wind was blowing, dropping the wind-chill temperature to almost 100 F (-37 C) below. Mushers typically have the best boots and parkas this side of the moon, but not even the best gear can keep out the most severe cold. King froze quickly.

He had mushed out fast, taking the lead in the first 100 miles (161 km). The conditions were brutal, and King didn't want to stop and peel off the mitten to check out his hand. He didn't feel any pain, or sense being colder in the hand than in the air, so he figured it was warm enough.

"The rest of me got so cold I couldn't detect the cold in my hand," he said.

King passed over Rosebud Summit on the far side of Angel Creek and made his first camp. The winds were horrendous. He had paused for a six-hour break, still leading, when Dave Monson passed him. But King felt good about where he was in the race. Resting, his body warmed up, King prepared to hit the trail. It dawned on him that he might want to take a closer look at the hand.

King had worn a cotton glove underneath the special mitten, and when he tried to remove it, it wouldn't budge. He struggled and gradually realized the problem. "It was frozen to my skin on the tips of the fingers," he recalled. "The glove was literally attached to my fingers. I thought, 'Wow, that can't be good.'" King inched the glove off his hand and when it was bare, the fingers were as white and waxy as candle sticks.

He bundled up again and resumed mushing. When King reached Mile 101 on the Steese Highway, he saw the wife of musher Dave Sawatzky. She was a nurse from Healy, Alaska, who was familiar with King's injury and knew about the warnings he had received from doctors about frostbite danger. King parked his dogs and walked up to her saying, "Jeannie, I'm worried about my hand."

Although the hand didn't hurt — it was numb — King removed the mitten and showed her his hand. Instantly, she grabbed it in both of her hands, pressed it against her chest, and said, "Oh, my God, Jeff." He had been matter of fact when he approached, but now he was alarmed. "It was very powerful," he said of her reaction. "She shook her head in disbelief, and I knew that I was screwed." Medical professionals later told him that the damage was so severe that he might lose some digits.

The Quest was over for King only about 100 miles (161 km) into the race. He scratched, telephoned his wife, Donna Gates, an artist who has painted several pictures featured in the official Quest race posters, and got a ride home. The next day he was at a hospital. The doctor who inspected his hand looked him in the eye and said,

"This is very serious. You're so lucky you can't feel. It is so frozen that it is now a wonderful gift to you because this would hurt like hell."

Simply warming the hand was insufficient treatment. King lost the tips of several fingers. He calls his hand "deformed" and says what nails he has are "ugly." Healing took a long time, but King never seriously considered retiring from mushing. More than twenty years later, he has put his left hand through trial after trial in the Quest and Iditarod. He never regained full feeling, strength, or sensitivity in that hand and he's convinced he did more damage by freezing it in the 1988 race than in the initial accident.

"It functions," he said of his left hand. But he must be more aware of cold on the trail, something that he says has become "second nature."

The father of three girls, King recalls that "as my children grew up, they complained that I would squeeze their hands too hard to cross the street. I couldn't tell how much pressure I was exerting. They always wanted to hold my right hand, not my left."

Finger dexterity is important to mushers. On the sled, it helps to maintain a good grip on the handlebars, but more significantly, it is important in feeding and caring for dogs at checkpoints. Mushers typically strip off bulky mittens and perform those critical tasks with bare fingers.

Sonny Lindner, who continues to compete in long-distance races in his sixties, said people have no idea what it takes to function in severely cold weather. "The cold comes through every seam or pinhole in your gear. The sled doesn't slide quite as well because the snow feels more like sand. Everything takes longer," said Lindner, "You're using your bare hands. You might stop what you're doing for a minute and stick them in your pocket, and then try again ...You have to be more careful for yourself and your dogs. A full-blown sprint would freeze their lungs. Every time you try to make food for the dogs, you start with a block of meat frozen at 50 (F) below."

While King was extra cautious, keeping his damaged hand warm, he didn't let it interfere with success. He was the runner-up to Quest champion Bruce Johnson in 1986 and finished third in 1987 when Bill Cotter won. Monson won the 1988 race when King was sidelined by the frozen hand. But with his goal of victory in a Quest unfulfilled, King prepared to enter again in 1989.

And then things got worse.

Roughly seven weeks before the start of the Quest — the date of January 4, 1989 is imprinted on King's mind — his three-story home burned down. King was not there, having been invited to a friend's house for dinner while his wife and daughters were out of town. King had left Hickory, a prized leader, and Snickers, an exceptionally fast runner, inside the house after a training run that day. Both dogs died in the blaze. "It was a huge blow," King said. When a cold snap hit the Alaska Interior, King was further demoralized, and his desire to compete plummeted lower than the temperature. But his wife urged him to carry through with his race plan for 1989. He borrowed two leaders named Molar and Hickey, the latter a Joe Runyan leader that had starred in Runyan's 1985 championship team.

The race, with forty-three mushers, began in Whitehorse that year. One of the competitors was Jeninne Cathers. At eighteen, she was the youngest-ever entrant. "I can't believe how relaxed I am," she said at the start. Usually, rookies are nervous wrecks, frazzled from last-minute preparations as they prepare to race into the great unknown.

Trail and weather conditions dictate each Quest. Even the most experienced mushers can be caught off guard by those two circumstances and have their race plans diverted. Only a day into the race, two mushers encountered unexpected open water. Amy Squibb of Fairbanks and Bob Graweher of Whitehorse both risked death when they, their bodies, dogs, and sleds were soaked on the way to Dawson City. They were lucky it was only minus 15 F (-26 C) degrees at the time. The two mushers had to build fires to warm themselves after performing self-rescues and later dried their gear in a Carmacks, Yukon laundry.

The trail was rough, and many mushers had to make repairs to damaged sleds. Ralph Seekins, a Fairbanks automobile dealer, had another problem. One of his dogs was knocked unconscious when it barked up the wrong tree. "She was so stunned, it looked like she'd been hit by a 300-pound tackle on a football field," said Seekins.

King set out with the leaders, his left hand protected by a new gizmo. He not only wore heavy mittens on the trail, but when resting indoors he kept a sleeve on that arm for additional warmth. Any type of cold still bothered the impaired hand.

King was first into Dawson City, the halfway mark, and was presented with four ounces of gold. The race remained tight, with Gerald Riley trailing by half an hour. Also in the hunt were Lindner; Kate Persons of Kotzebue, Alaska; Bruce Lee, a close friend of King's from Denali Park; and Vern Halter of Trapper Creek, Alaska.

Riley suggested that observers not be fooled — that the Quest was King's race to win. "Jeff's just playing with me," Riley said, "Every time I stop to rest he passes me by."

A resident of Nenana, a small town on the Tanana River about 60 miles (97 km) south of Fairbanks, Riley was the first musher to consider seriously racing in the Quest and the Iditarod in the same season. Running two 1,000-mile (1,609-km) races a few weeks apart generally was thought to be too much for human stamina and, beyond question too much for sled dogs.

Riley entered both events in 1989, using twelve dogs for the Quest and planning to use different dogs for the Iditarod. Riley, then fifty-two, said he had borrowed the Quest dogs from Native villagers and was saving his own, better dogs for the Iditarod. It would be a unique feat, but Riley said he was doing it more for the potential financial reward than anything else. "Who wouldn't want to try for double the prize money?" he asked.

Musher Tom Randall of Whitehorse made a comment that symbolized just how far-fetched Riley's scheme seemed at the time:

"Go on the Quest. Go on the Iditarod. Then keep going to Russia."
Riley didn't fulfill his dream. He was disqualified from the Quest.
But the idea of doing two marathon races in the same winter began
percolating in others' minds.

The layover in Dawson was pleasant enough. But soon after
resuming the race, King's sled fell into open water on the Yukon
River, dunking him neck deep in the dark. Using the sled as a raft,
King held tight to the handlebars with one hand and paddled with
the other. Pulling himself out of the water in the minus 30 F (-1 C)
temperature, King was freezing and focused on finding a warm
place to dry off. He found it at a cabin 15 miles (24 km) away.
Behind King, many of the other leaders took the same fall. They
were far enough apart from one another that no one saw others
fall in. They were risking their lives, but all survived, and shook
off their shivers as they raced onward to the cabin owned by Gar
Guimond, a former Quest competitor.

"I was more frightened than wet," Vern Halter said.

Oddly enough, this near disaster didn't even rearrange the
leaders. Each musher took about a six-hour break at the cabin in
order to rest, recover, and warm up. King stayed near the front of
the pack and with 45 miles (72 km) left, he had regained the lead.
As he mushed from Two Rivers onto the Chena River and into
downtown Fairbanks, he worked his dogs through a heavy
snowstorm. Pushing hard, it was enough to best Halter, who
finished in second place 20 minutes behind, and Jim Wilson of Fort
Yukon, Alaska who finished third another 45 minutes back.

The payoff was $20,000, and King appreciated every penny.
He could put a roof on his new house.

CHAPTER SIX

OF CINNAMON ROLLS AND OTHER TREATS

"...the Klondike grew into a national mania. Perhaps 100,000 people would join the chase, risking everything for passage to the territories of Alaska and the Yukon."
— John Balzar, *Yukon Alone*

2009 The night sky was brightened by what seemed like a million stars outside the Braeburn Lodge, the first checkpoint on the 2009 Yukon Quest, 100 trail miles (152 km) from Whitehorse. The checkers stoked a barrel fire behind the lodge, sending smoke signals to mushers as they approached. It was minus 30F (-34 C) degrees.

It had been all fanfare and festivities in Whitehorse as race fans cheered the mushers on their way out of town. But as the sun went down and the teams veered into the woods, the race was all business. Unlike the Iditarod, it was easy for fans and handlers driving mushers' trucks to follow the early-going on the road. When John Firth served as president of the Quest's Canadian board of directors in the mid-1990s, he urged a fine-tuning of the trail departing from the start so spectators could watch more of the race.

"We tried to promote more," Firth said. "We set up the early miles for maximum exposure. It clicked. There were people for the first fifteen or twenty miles. It exposed more of the race to the people."

On the outskirts of Whitehorse, the road turns onto the Klondike Highway and for motorists it was a straight shot to the Braeburn Lodge. Inside, a race chalkboard leaned against a wall and was filled in with times as each competitor arrived.

Braeburn Lodge is renowned for the bulk of its food portions. It is as if any order is appropriately sized for a competitive eating contest. The famous cinnamon rolls, about three inches thick and as big around as a hubcap, are a bargain at $8.50 Canadian. The cheeseburgers, priced at $11, contain a half-pound of meat and are as big around as a spare tire. The grilled cheese sandwiches approximate the size of Sponge Bob Squarepants' butt and easily serve four. The Braeburn Lodge does its bit for world peace because it makes people share.

After parking their dogs following ten or more hours on the trail, some mushers feed their own appetites with Braeburn goodies. Bill Cotter, entered in the Quest's companion 300-mile race (482-km) in addition to renting a team to Japanese musher Yuka Honda for the long race, inhaled a bowl of New England clam chowder. Though describing the container as a bowl hardly does it justice. It was more like a bucket of soup.

In the first Quest, when organizers were preoccupied with making the race as tough as possible, the Braeburn Lodge was off-limits to mushers. "You had to camp across the street," Cotter said. "No food." A weary Cotter could not finish his soup.

The top three mushers in the full Quest arrived in mid-evening, Jean-denis Britten of Dawson City, Martin Buser, and Luc Tweddell, a rookie from Whitehorse, all declared a rest. However, Jon Little kept on going. His boldness made him the race leader.

PEOPLE HAD mixed opinions about how well Buser would do in his first Quest. With his record of four championships in the Iditarod, some believed he would blow away this field. Others felt he was in for a dose of humility adapting to the peculiar difficulties of the Quest. Buser never had been on this trail and was used to the Iditarod where the twenty-six checkpoints averaged fifty miles apart. The Quest has just ten checkpoints and includes a 201-mile (323 km) doozy of a stretch between Pelly Crossing and Dawson City.

Buser acted the role of gracious, humble newcomer, repeatedly referring to himself as a rookie, never for a moment playing the role of a big shot. When asked if he thought he could win, Buser demurred. He said every time he enters a race he thinks he has a chance. It was a non-answer answer. At the Quest kickoff banquet, Buser even made fun of his rookie status. After weaving his way through tables to the stage in order to pick up his start number, he joked, "This rookie doesn't know his way to the podium. Hopefully, I can find the starting line — and the finish."

Buser found the starting line okay and got off to a fast start. With clear weather and an impeccably groomed trail, the dogs moved comfortably between Whitehorse and Braeburn. This was notable because there had been many complaints about a letdown in trail care the year before. Race manager Doug Grilliot said that improvement was a point of emphasis for 2009.

"It had fallen a little bit below what a professional sled-dog race should be," Grilliot admitted.

A minimum effort is expected from trail-breakers at the start of a race and between checkpoints. But if the race starts and a storm dumps feet of fresh snow, the wind blows, or it warms up and rains, then mushers are on their own. "You can't control Mother Nature," Grilliot said.

In a way, that's what mushers and dogs are trying to do, or at least tame it for a little while.

Behind Braeburn Lodge, a flat, snow-covered field provided considerable room for resting. Full teams stretched out in rows, as if they were crops that had been planted. There was sufficient room for veterinarians to walk among the dogs and check out each one carefully.

Lance mapped out a strategy for Jason that would enable him to contend for the crown. "I feel like I got a team that's capable of competing," Jason Mackey said, "if I can stick to the schedule." That didn't take into account that in at least one man's view, Jason, thirty-seven, was really seventy-five. A baffled race fan in Whitehorse thought Jason must be Dick, the boys' father. Of course, after several hundred miles of sleep deprivation and winter weather, all of the mushers' bodies started feeling about seventy-five years old.

Little, the genial former newspaperman, was as frisky as his dogs, barely stopping for a hello at Braeburn. While others halted, perhaps finding it impossible to drive on by without ingesting a cinnamon roll, Little set up camp on the trail. Resting in privacy added a shroud of mystery to his strategy.

It was nice to be in the lead, Little said, but the Quest isn't a hundred-mile race, it's a 1,000-mile (1,609 km) race. Ask him later — much later — how he was doing.

CHAPTER SEVEN

MYSTERIOUS BUSH MAN

"The man who turns his back on the comforts of an elder civilization, to face the savage youth, the primordial simplicity of the North, may estimate success at an inverse ratio to the quantity and quality of his hopelessly fixed habits." — Jack London, *In a Far Country*

1990-1993 The Bush rat who had come north from North Carolina was almost a hermit in the woods off the Alaska road system, living in a tent with his trap-line dogs, foregoing the neatness of haircuts, eschewing the trappings of electricity. No one was going to bump into Charlie Boulding by accident and he wasn't accepting phone calls.

His hair was graying and long, tied in braids, and he lived the pure life in the wilderness, rarely speaking of what he had left behind somewhere else. He was into middle-age, but when he started training and racing his sled dogs, adapting them to the trail from the wild, he spoke in expansive philosophy rather than terse sentences. And the people loved him for it, especially when he began to race fast and win titles.

Boulding was the epitome of what Yukon Quest creators had in mind. They wanted a long, tough race that tested woodsmen's skills, run by mushers with small bankrolls testing dogs hardened by rural living. Boulding had to do his own testing first, to change over from dogs used for hauling freight to dogs trained to run fast.

Boulding, who lived near Manley so rustically he didn't have four walls and a roof to warm him, nor indoor plumbing, was a curiosity when he appeared for his first Quest in 1989. He placed eleventh. A year later, he finished tenth. He was earning small paydays of a couple thousand dollars, and his mere presence added to the flavor of the race because he was a pleasant man and interesting to talk with. He was the genuine article, the Bush man who acted on the rural fantasy of a generation caught up in the hurly-burly of traffic jams, high costs of living, and other social pressures. Truthfully, there was a small part inside of many Quest fans that envied Boulding, even if they knew they could never be him.

Jeff King won his Quest championship, bad hand and all, in 1989, just edging Vern Halter. Then in 1990, they reversed places. Halter had his turn, winning by nearly three and a half hours. "I felt I should have won the race in 1989," Halter said. "I wanted a little revenge. The year I won the race I had a dominant dog team. That was a heck of a dog team. They were fun to drive the whole way."

Halter also had paid his dues. One year crossing over Eagle Summit, Halter was caught by howling winds and blowing snow along with King and Sonny Lindner. "Eagle Summit was bad news," he said. All three mushers turned back and sheltered in a cabin. The act of winning was as satisfying as the result of winning. "That was one of the most fun races of my career," he said.

Just before the 1990 race the temperature hit minus 60 F (-51 C) in the Fairbanks area. "Why do people live here?" asked race co-founder LeRoy Shank. He did not provide his own answer, only a smile.

By the time he arrived in Dawson City, Halter was running five hours ahead, but he riskily extended his rest because of a storm. He poured it on during the second half of the race and counting on his leader Nellie, Halter passed King for the last time with 75 miles (121 km) to go. Halter, who later moved to Willow, Alaska and became a tour operator, then was dividing his time between being a public defender in Kotzebue and training thirty-five dogs in Trapper Creek. He was a part-time lawyer and part-time musher. Halter, forty at the time, won $20,000 and set a race record from Fairbanks to Whitehorse of 11 days, 17 hours, 9 minutes.

The period between 1989 and 1995 was an intriguing time in long-distance mushing. Joe Runyan claimed the Yukon Quest crown in 1985. That was the year Libby Riddles became the first woman to win the Iditarod. Susan Butcher then won the Iditarod in 1986, 1987 and 1988. Her string was interrupted by Runyan, the 1989 champion. Butcher won again in 1990, but overcoming a violent storm on the Bering Sea coast in 1991 Rick Swenson notched his fifth win, still the record for most victories in the Iditarod.

At that time, a new 1,000-mile (1,609-km) mush was created in the interest of international harmony across the Bering Strait in Siberia. Named the Hope race, it attracted some participation from Alaskan mushers. Bob Holder, a Fairbanks well-digger, made his debut in the Quest with a twentieth-place finish in 1989. Six years later, after also dabbling in the Iditarod, Holder strung together a winter for the ages. He completed the Quest, the Iditarod, and the Hope race, back to back to back, running 3,000 miles (4,828 km) on the trail in the same winter. It was an unprecedented feat that never was duplicated because the Hope race soon folded. Holder placed eighth in the Quest, thirty-first in the Iditarod, and then kept on going. Originally from Havana, Florida, Holder started speaking a little bit of Russian with a Southern drawl. He had a dog truck with a sign "Bob Holder's Junk Yard Dogs" on the side and said he liked the idea of being a pioneer.

"I was thinking, 'Well, no one's ever done it,'" Holder said. "Before Columbus, no one had ever done that."

However, before Holder performed his triple, Boulding became the first musher to complete the Quest and Iditarod in the same year. That was 1992 when Boulding finished third in the Quest and forty-third in the Iditarod. By then, though, Boulding was already a Quest champion. He went from unknown to title-holder quickly, claiming first in the 1991 race.

It was a breakthrough race, not only for Boulding, but for the event, his suspenseful victory by five minutes over Bruce Lee of Denali Park establishing a historically fast time. At 10 days, 21 hours, 12 minutes, it was the first finish in less than eleven days.

Being a trapper and Bush liver, Boulding did not exactly reside at the epicenter of a cash economy. He remembered hearing when the Quest began and thinking he would like to do it, but he didn't have the bucks to enter. It took until 1989 for him to make his debut, and even then he was poorly equipped. When Boulding pulled into Whitehorse that year he blinked when he saw all of the fancy diesel trucks with dogs resting in boxes spiffy enough to be located in suburban subdivisions. Boulding's own dogs arrived sprawled on straw in the back of a Chevy Blazer. As he drove, some of the dogs stuck their heads out the back window.

"I was actually wanting to do the Quest before that," said Boulding. "But I didn't really have the money. It was a pretty low-budget operation."

Boulding had competed in some middle-distance races in the Alaska Interior, but he really had no idea how his dogs stacked up against teams training full-time. When he finished eleventh, with minimal preparation, he started believing he might be pretty good at the sport. A year later, in 1990, when Boulding finished tenth, "I realized that it could be profitable."

There are usually considerable distances between first place and tenth in the standings, but it is also a figurative distance. A champion musher needs the mindset, the readiness to win, to be willing to take chances when necessary and set the pace when appropriate. When the 1991 race began, Boulding, then forty-eight, wore his same old parka, patched where it had been torn, old mukluks that sagged around his feet, and he displayed no evidence of a corporate sponsor that specialized in the manufacture of high-tech winter gear.

As the race unfolded, Boulding went out at a swift pace, just hanging around the leaders. He didn't force the pace, but stayed in the shadow of more experienced Quest racers. In the minds of fans and other mushers Boulding was running a tenth-place team.. Everyone thought that when the racing got hot he would fade.

Boulding stuck with Lee, a long-time musher, and John Schandelmeier. Schandelmeier, like Boulding, was coming off a middling finish. He was twelfth the year before.

Lee's first Quest was in 1986 when he also placed twelfth. Lee had traveled by dog-team extensively in the Brooks Range, along the Kobuk River, in Kotzebue, all over Alaska's North Slope, and in Denali Park, but for the joy of the trips. When he moved to Denali Park, he started taking sled-dog trips with Jeff King and another friend, Ed Foran, both of whom were training for the Quest. They encouraged him to enter the race. "It's a great adventure," Lee remembers Foran saying.

One day Lee and King drove into Fairbanks for some business, and King pulled up to the Quest office. "Let's go in and sign you up today," King said. So at thirty-two Lee became a Quest racer. And his friends had not been fibbing, either. The Quest was a grand adventure compared to recreational mushing.

"It totally reopened my eyes to what the dogs could do," Lee said. "It was like the difference between playing baseball in the back yard, playing catch with dad and playing Major League Baseball where all at once the other people are pulling different strategies on you. Like most rookies, I pulled so many bonehead moves. Looking back, I could have been in the top five in that first race, but I just didn't know what I was doing."

Years later, Lee laughed about all of the errors a more seasoned musher would never make. He didn't know how to handle sleep deprivation, he said. He didn't know the trail. He didn't know the smart places to stop. He earned the dunce cap, he added, when he took a six-hour rest when he was only fifteen minutes shy of Dawson City and the mandatory 36-hour rest required there.

Pals King and Foran gave Lee a notebook's worth of advice, but once he started getting tired he forgot as much as he recalled. In 1988, Lee returned and placed fourth. In 1989, he finished third. The biggest challenge in his early races was figuring out how to keep his mind sharp and to avoid falling asleep at an inconvenient time.

In the process, Lee collected a storehouse of hallucination stories. He found himself dozing off on the back of the sled, jerking his head up and to the side to duck away from a tree limb that didn't exist. Frequently, he heard things. Lee had complete conversations with people who were not present on the trail. It kept happening until he almost drove himself nuts. Other times mushing through the night he would hear his name called. "Hey, Bruce!" someone would shout. "Of course there was nobody there. I was in the middle of the Yukon River."

What transformed Lee from a musher just trying to finish into a musher who could contend for the championship was his ability to adapt to lack of sleep. He realized that the sleep problem was multi-faceted. Not only was he truly tired, but it affected his mood. The sleep made him manic. For a while when he was really worn down he got depressed. Then after he slept he became deliriously happy.

"So what you gain is the experience of when those down moments come," Lee said. "I thought, 'Boy, I'll be glad when this is over because I know that an hour from now I'm going to be really on top of things again.' That's why mushers set schedules. You start out-thinking yourself. You think you're doing worse than you are."

The highs, though, are equally high. "There's a moment of ecstasy coming somewhere," Lee said. "You'll pull into a checkpoint and see friendly faces. There's going to be a moment in the middle of the night when your dogs seem like they're just running strong and you've got a million-dollar-run when the moon's out and the northern lights are out and you think, 'I am the luckiest person in the world to be out here seeing this.' The thing is not to quit in those other moments."

In the 1991 race, Lee was convinced he was headed for a different moment of ecstasy — the champion's prize. However, Lee admitted he was like most mushers just learning about Charlie Boulding. He didn't take his capabilities seriously. Boulding did not have the fanciest, up-to-date gear. Heck, Boulding was only months shy of turning forty-nine and at that time no one of that age was winning long-distance races.

"He's a great personality," Lee said. "I love the guy. But at first it was, 'Who is this guy?' I just didn't take him seriously when

I should have buried him. Then things equaled out as we went down the trail."

Lee, Schandelmeier, and Boulding ran close together as the Quest approached Fairbanks. Spectators lined the route near Nordale Road in Two Rivers, and Lee's dogs spooked themselves into a tangle. In the time it took for Lee to reorganize his team, Boulding put on a push. Lee overcame Schandelmeier, but couldn't regain that lost five minutes on Boulding.

"I was just the newcomer and they sort of wrote me off," Boulding said of Lee and Schandelmeier. "I'd been running behind them for three or four days and I realized I had a faster dog team than either of them. They didn't."

Boulding actually toyed with moving earlier, of taking the lead into Circle City and running all of the way to Angel Creek without a rest. But he worried that he would take too much out of his dogs too soon and get caught in a storm on Eagle Summit.

"If I got to Eagle Summit and there was a big blow — which I had experienced one other year — I knew they would catch me up and I would be dead in my tracks," Boulding said. "I thought my dogs were faster so I would wait until the end."

When Boulding turned on the afterburners, he said, a spectator on the road clocked his dogs moving at fifteen mph. It was extraordinary.

Boulding, the low-maintenance Bush dweller, won $25,000 for first place. But he had a pledge going into the race from dog-food manufacturer Royal Canin that if he won, the company would match his winnings. The sponsor paid off. Suddenly, Boulding recognized he could make a lot more money mushing than trapping.

By then, too, he had a volunteer handler, Robin Morrison, who became his wife, and a cabin had replaced his tent. The real secret behind Boulding's early success was simple. He had not just been running heavy-duty trap-line dogs. His dogs' lineage traced to the sprint teams of Fairbanks musher Curtis Erhart.

"We were ahead of the curve for a few years," Boulding said. "They were fast dogs."

More aggravating by far for Lee was that Boulding told everyone before the race that he was going to sleep six to eight hours every night. Lee said, "Not in this race." But Boulding got his beauty sleep and won anyway. At the finish when Boulding was asked how he was going to spend his newfound bounty, he said he just might invest in a new parka.

Boulding's popularity in the Bush increased after his victory, where he had an image that included the nickname, "Good-time Charlie." However, Boulding said his first move after collecting his prize money was to see his lawyer and accountant. "I may seem like an illiterate country boy, but I'm not dumb," he said.

No one who talked to Boulding for five minutes would take him for dumb, but the 1991 race was probably the last time he was underestimated. A little bit of his life story leaked out, too, after he became Quest champ. He had been married twice before coming to Alaska, been trained as a Green Beret in the Army, fathered three grown children, lived in South Dakota and Wyoming and worked as a construction superintendent. In the continental U.S. and in Nenana, where he first lived in Alaska, Boulding came to appreciate the Sioux and Athabascan Indian cultures.

He had had troubles with alcohol, too, and living in the Bush, along the Tanana River, with no neighbors for miles and responding only to the fishing seasons when salmon swam through and got caught in his fish wheel, produced a more peaceful lifestyle. Boulding and Robin had met when she was twenty-three, half of his age at the time, and he picked her up hitchhiking on his way to a dog race in Coldfoot. They became a permanent team.

Boulding was chasing a repeat in 1992 when he returned to the Quest, but finished third behind Schandelmeier and Sonny Lindner. A race official told Boulding they were holding him at a checkpoint because of a vet's concern about the health of one dog. Later, Boulding said the vet had told officials there was no reason for worry. "That took me out of it," Boulding said.

The situation firmed up Boulding's resolve for 1993. Seeking to become the first musher to capture two Quest crowns, Boulding cruised to the $25,000 first prize 3 hours, 31 minutes ahead of Bruce Johnson and said he never worried. "It was too easy," Boulding said. "I was even lollygagging at the end.".

Boulding, no longer an unknown, received royal receptions at some checkpoints. One sign read, "Eagle Loves Charlie." Dennis Layton, who operated the community grocery store, said, "It is like he's one of us. He could move here and fit right in."

After his second Quest triumph, Boulding became a full-time Iditarod musher and capped a string of top-ten finishes with a best finish of third in 1998.

In the early 2000s, as he passed his sixtieth birthday, Boulding gave up long-distance mushing. He had had a bout with colon cancer and beat the illness, but his knees were creaky and his back often ached on the trail. He kept eight dogs from his kennel and sold the rest.

Charlie and Robin Boulding invested in a time-share sailboat that they used for a couple of months a year in the Caribbean. Boulding has immersed himself with a cross-section of technology that provides readouts on wind and weather and maps.

Boulding also kept the old homestead. There, the Bouldings are raising a baby daughter who is approximately sixty-five years younger than her father. Although he still rarely visits cities, once in a while Boulding ventures into some of the small Alaska villages not far from home.

There he is still recognized. "To them," Boulding said, "I'm Charlie Boulding, the Quest champion."

CHAPTER EIGHT

DANGER AND TRAGEDY

"Their (moose) eyesight is poor. Their demeanor is stubborn. These two traits combine to make them regard anything that approaches as an adversary."
— Ann Mariah Cook, *Running North*

1992-1993 You used to hear stories about traveling carnivals with wrestling bears. Declawed and muzzled, Bruno went one-on-one with drunk or delusional men drawn from the crowd and typically pinned them flat on the canvas.

Such man-versus-beast encounters have faded from the live-entertainment circuit. It is difficult to recall the last time one heard about such a confrontation between human and an extra-large member of the animal kingdom — except for those who followed the 1993 Yukon Quest. One of northern poet Robert Service's most famous lines is his mention of strange things occurring under the midnight sun. Well, not even Service imagined what took place on a remote stretch of trail between thirty-four-year-old musher Jeff Mann of Mentasta, Alaska and a ticked-off moose.

This was no stage show, either. Mushing from Circle to Angel Creek, on the Alaskan side of the Quest, Charlie Boulding, and Jay Cadzow — the uncle of young Josh Cadzow making his Quest debut in 2009 — encountered a cow moose on the trail. Carefully, the dog drivers worked their way around the animal and continued racing, though Cadzow flung a fireball made from dog booties doused with fuel towards the moose as a distraction.

Somewhat later on the same day, an unaware Mann paused in the same area, about five miles short of Angel Creek, to splash water on his face at an open stream. When he looked up, an angry moose faced him and his dogs. "There were these distinctly green eyes about seven and a half feet (2.3 meters) off the ground," Mann recounted.

Quest rules require that mushers transport a variety of mandatory gear in their sleds at all times and must be prepared to show the items at checkpoints. However, coming into Carmacks, Mann realized he was missing his ax. Before checking in, he parked his sled and ran to the local store and for $30 purchased a new ax with a three-foot-long handle. The theory behind carrying an ax is that it will come in handy for chopping wood in case there is a need for an emergency fire. It is doubtful that race officials pictured the ax used as a weapon.

When the moose came after Mann and his dogs, furious at his intrusion into her territory, the ax was his only protection. Moose can weigh 1,200 pounds (545 kilos), (though this one was clearly in need of food and weighed less). When angered, moose rear up and can pummel a man or other animal with their hooves. A dazed and fatigued Mann, in disbelief realized he was in for a battle.

"I said 'buddy, it's either you or me,'" Mann recalled, "'and you are going down.' It was like Tarzan in the Arctic." Mann versus moose. The musher swung his ax and dodged the hooves. For a half-hour, the confrontation raged until Mann chopped the moose down to size.

"He and I were nose to nose," Mann said. "I kind of cut off his snout. Now he's standing there with this gaping wound and a flopping nose, and I'm thinking, 'Holy cow, this is for real.' We parlayed almost like a boxing match. I was faking a right and he was ducking a right."

As his energy rapidly faded, Mann looked for a weak spot. He aimed the blunt end of the ax at the moose's head and bashed it. The smash between the eyes cracked the animal's skull. It fell to its knees and then the exhausted, sweaty, and blood-covered Mann cut its throat. "And that's all she wrote," he said.

In accordance with Alaska state law, Mann had to dress out and remove the moose meat. He did so, but the bones remained in the trail. At least until two unhappy mushers, John Peep of Fairbanks, and Hans Gatt, had to drive their sleds over what was left of the moose.

Mann mushed on to the Angel Creek checkpoint and took a break, sitting in boots and outer garb stained from moose blood. Shaken, Mann felt lucky to be alive and uninjured. People who heard the story were astonished, agreeing that it was one of the strangest occurrences ever on the Yukon Quest trail.

Things could have been worse. On the Canadian side, mushers had been warned about a mother grizzly bear roaming around with two cubs. It would have taken more than an ax for Mann or any other musher to talk their way out of that showdown.

Mann's meeting with the moose underscored how lucky Boulding and Cadzow had been to avoid the animal. If Boulding had become embroiled in a life-or-death contest, he might not have won the 1993 race.

Although Boulding thought he should have won three Quests in a row from 1991 to 1993, it was John Schandelmeier who won the 1992 crown. Schandelmeier was a role-model Quest participant. A musher with a small kennel who lived in Paxson more than 250 miles (402 km) by road from Anchorage where he grew up, Schandelmeier was admired for his bush-craft and know-how.

In his sixth Quest, Schandelmeier tried some unorthodox approaches. The image of long-distance race dogs to people who don't live in the north is stuck in the past when huge Malamutes pulled freight sleds and gorgeous-looking black and white Siberian huskies ran in harness. Once mushers conquered the unknown trails of the Iditarod and Quest, however, they looked for innovative ways to reduce their times.

A dog known as the Alaskan husky emerged. It is not a registered breed, but a mix of several types of dogs raised for racing in snow country. Schandelmeier, then thirty-nine, decided to breed more speed into his team by mating German shepherds with his huskies. The prevailing theory was that it was important to put long distances on a team during the training season. Instead, Schandelmeier cut his training base from 1,500 miles to 900 (2,413 km to 1,448). While others became fixated on stamina, he counted on speed.

The plan worked perfectly. "We're dealing with training muscles, whether that's human, horses or dogs doesn't make any difference," Schandelmeier said. "I train to build muscle tone. I'm a firm believer in having happy dogs and not putting a lot of pressure on them."

Schandelmeier's dogs seemed happy enough trotting across the landscape, and so did he when they finished first in Whitehorse. Jeff Mann had been labeled a Zen musher because of his interest in Oriental philosophy, but Schandelmeier seemed more Zen-like at the time. His best memories transcend victory.

Schandelmeier said he likes to be thought of as a hard-working musher with wise training methods. "I want people to remember that 'He's a dog trainer,' " Schandelmeier said of himself, "that 'he can get the best out of his dogs.' There are no major tricks. It takes a lot of patience."

Although Schandelmeier gained pleasure from winning the Quest, the actual moment of crossing the finish line ahead of everyone else did not produce his most satisfying race moments. One of those, he said, came in a race in which Eagle Summit was battered by bad weather. Four other dog teams stalled on the hill. Those dogs wouldn't budge, but his dogs would. "They were all faster than me," Schandelmeier said. "I had a really nice, steady dog team. I had to pull them (the other teams) over the summit. That was pretty satisfying. That means more to me than winning."

Schandelmeier did not defend his title in 1993, but the rookie of the year in that race was Jay Cadzow, who finished fifth.

In '93, the older Cadzow, who helped his nephew train for the Quest sixteen years later, dodged the moose that gave Mann so much trouble, and showed off a solid running team of dogs with a hodge-podge of backgrounds. They were not even all his. Sled-dog owners in Fort Yukon and the surrounding area had pooled their teams for him. In order for Cadzow to afford the entry fee, the costs of travel and racing, neighbors held bake sales and raffles, auctioned off hand-made fur hats and held fund-raising dinners. This is a traditional way of doing business in Bush Alaska, off the road system. There is a long history of village Natives backing a single musher with their resources.

Cadzow wore Army-Navy surplus wool winter clothing, not a brand-name parka and boots, and said the only new item of equipment he bought with the proceeds of village help was a sled. Cadzow not only posted his high finish, he also earned respect in another way, earning the $1,000 Alyeska Vets Choice Award for his dog care.

THAT 1993 QUEST was Bruce Johnson's last. Not because he retired, either.

The thickly bearded, personable Johnson, who moved north from Montana and settled in British Columbia, skipped several Quests after his triumph. But he returned to finish second in 1993. Johnson planned to compete in the 1994 race, too. However, in November of 1993, the mushing world was shocked when Johnson, forty-eight, the married father of three grown children, drowned along with a team of eight dogs after plunging through thin ice on Lake Atlin near his home   .

There were no witnesses to his second training run of the day on the evening of November 22, when Johnson, mushing a team of young dogs, perished in a scenario that provokes fear among long-distance dogdrivers. It is not easy for a musher to tell if ice is thick enough to hold him and a sled. Speculation was that Johnson's team might have been spooked and dragged him farther out onto ice where he would not have otherwise ventured. But there was no proof. The Royal Canadian Mounted Police recovered Johnson's body and he was cremated.

Despite the dangers and close calls from extreme temperatures, howling winds, devastating storms and false ice covering, no musher in the Iditarod or Quest has ever died. Johnson is the only one to die while training for one of the events.

Mushers who raced with and against Johnson still remember him fondly. Calling Johnson a good friend, Jeff King said the men spent considerable time on the trail in early Quests. "I borrowed dogs from him and loaned him dogs," King said. "He was just a real stand-up guy — never a whiner, never complaining about anything. Just a wonderful, wonderful guy. I liked Bruce a lot."

Frank Turner, dean of Canadian long-distance mushers, was close to Johnson and at the time of his death took a helicopter above the lake to try to reconstruct what happened. He said the reason for Johnson and the dogs going a mile out on the lake despite its iffy surface remains a mystery. Perhaps the young dogs panicked for an unknown reason. Johnson was renowned for being savvy around lakes and river ice, so it was even more perplexing for him to die in such a manner, Turner said.

"Bruce was one of my best friends," he said.

Turner said he obtained many of his first groups of dogs from Johnson. Turner described Johnson as a man of generous spirit, who even in the middle of a race stopped to talk to people at their trail cabins, regularly visiting one family that produced homemade ice cream. The family also made mittens, hats and socks, and Johnson gathered up the goods, sold them at the Quest finisher's banquet, and then sent the money back.

"I traveled quite a bit with him," Turner said, "and I can never remember Bruce going by a cabin that had a light on and not stopping, even if it was to have a quick drink or tea, but just to thank the people for being there for the mushers."

Turner began his own long-distance mushing for fun, not accomplishment, but his team kept improving. Johnson relentlessly teased him about being too cautious, too much of a fuddy-duddy on the trail. His dogs, Johnson said, were too good for him. "He said I didn't push them enough," Turner said, "and that I should have finished better. He would say it in a humorous way, so it wasn't hurtful to me. It was the truth and I knew that. And I did eventually win the race. It was terrible when Bruce died. I never go on a river now, especially in the beginning of winter, when I don't think about Bruce. When I think of Bruce now, it means I am extremely safe."

In a sport where the competitors race well into middle age, many still-active entrants in the Quest and Iditarod knew Johnson. Those too new and too young to have raced with him know the story of how he died and it serves as a reminder that they can't be too careful. That is Johnson's legacy.

CHAPTER NINE

A PLACE TO CATCH SOME SHUT EYE

"The mail route was the only highway in those days, open as soon as the ice was stable enough in fall and there until it began to break up in spring. On it, the dogsled mailmen were the sole link between Dawson City, Fortymile, Eagle, and the Alaskan Interior."
— Adam Killick, *Racing the White Silence*

2009 Rarely will any checkpoint in any race be as hospitable to weary mushers as Pelly Crossing. A speck of a place on the map, Pelly Crossing is a cluster of buildings along the Klondike Highway between Whitehorse and Dawson City, but it has a community hall large enough for public meetings and dances. For one or two nights a year, it is for some mushers a home away from home.

An inviting stop, Pelly Crossing was set up with long tables and chairs, electricity for reporters and photographers sending race coverage worldwide, cloistered areas to throw a sleeping bag, and even a handful of couches. Anyone lucky enough to score one could approximate a hotel-quality cushy sleep. The room was well heated and the heavy exterior clothing necessary to repel the northern cold could be dispensed with.

Even better for those with an appetite, the locals put on a hunger-satiating memorable feed. For $10 Canadian, a musher, handler, race official, reporter, or fan could inhale a hearty dinner. The menu offered turkey, gravy, dressing, corn, a roll and a slice of fruit pie. Good thing the huskies weren't allowed in since they need 10,000 calories a day on the trail.

Between bites of his meal, race judge Thomas Tetz, the former competitor, and one of the transplanted Germans, tried to explain why the Quest and the Yukon appeal so much to his countrymen and other outsiders. "The Yukon," he said, "reminds people of what they don't have — open spaces." The romance of the race is wrapped up in images of the cold, snow, the wilderness, remoteness, pristine territory, and frontier history. It was as succinct evaluation as one could find.

Pelly Crossing was a smart place to recharge. There was time for a nap, to ingest caloric fuel, to prepare for the long road ahead. After this pause, the trail wound past the Stewart River and disappeared off the highway and into the woods. Although there were places where dogs might be dropped, there was no official checkpoint for another 201 miles (323 km). Pelly Crossing to Dawson City is a crucial stretch in the Quest. The fastest musher between these checkpoints would not clinch the race, but a musher could lose the race with a major mistake if the terrain were not approached seriously.

WAYNE HALL, fifty-seven, is the kind of musher that Quest organizers love. Hall and his wife Scarlett live in a remote cabin. He enters the Quest when he can afford it. The years he doesn't enter, Scarlett operates the race checkpoint in their hometown of Eagle. Or, as Hall put it, some years she manages the checkpoint, and the rest of the time she manages him.

Hall has never been a contender. A long-time trapper, he is switching his primary business focus over to tourism. That would be summer tourism since the Top of the World Highway from Dawson City into Eagle is covered with mounds of snow and closed in winter.

One of Hall's favorite books is *The Worst Journey in the World*, an adventure story about Antarctica written by Cherry Aspland-Garrard, a survivor of Robert Falcon Scott's ill-fated South Pole expedition, which describes severe cold that is familiar to Hall. Just weeks before the Quest, when the Yukon and Alaska were in the grip of a deep freeze, the temperature in Eagle dropped to minus 70 F (-57 C). "The part of Alaska we live in is the hottest part and the coldest part," Hall said. Quest temperatures were in the minus 20s, almost tropical to him, and Hall wore blue jeans under his snowsuit.

Every corner of the Pelly Crossing community hall was staked out. The most remote spot, behind a curtain, was designated for mushers. They staggered in, gulped a meal, and slept. Jamaican musher Newton Marshall was groggy. Bill Cotter stripped off his outer gear and hung a parka and boots on wall hooks to drip dry. Other mushers did the same.

In late evening, a discouraged Jean-denis Britten of Dawson pulled on his trail gear. He sat on a chair and slipped on his boots. Britten, who had dropped three dogs after his quick start, said he was going to mush home and drop out of the race there. In 2008, he placed ninth and won $8,000. That finish had given him hope of contending in 2009. Now his race had blown up.

Britten was advised to shift fresh dogs into lead. Just maybe the new dogs would revive his chances. The pep talk did nothing for Britten. "I don't want to be twentieth," he said. Still, he announced he was going back out. But eight hours later, at 7 a.m., as breakfast was served, there was Britten, still wearing his cold-weather gear, standing around the community hall. He was the first to scratch. "You can make all the plans you want," he said dispiritedly.

And you end up a footnote.

There was one major difference from the year before. As Grilliot promised, extra care had been taken with the trail. Mushers who had complained about potholes large enough to eat a sled in 2008, raved about the smooth quality of the trail a year later. "It's the fastest trail I've ever been on in the Quest," said three-time champion Hans Gatt. Front-of-the-pack racer Hugh Neff did Gatt one better. "This is the best trail I've ever seen in any race I've ever been on," Neff said.

The community hall turkey dinner was so popular that the food ran out before late-arriving mushers could partake. It wasn't bad enough that mushers at the back of the pack were actually at the back of the pack, now they missed out on what was probably the best full-course meal available along the trail. There were no Sonny Lindners among them with surf-and-turf selections in their sleds.

When Colleen Robertia, the rookie from Kasilof, Alaska, the Kenai Peninsula town well-represented by Jason Mackey and Jon Little, came through the front door she was greeted by a sign reading, "Canteen Closed." Robertia strode behind the counter, rummaged for leftovers, and spooned out some lukewarm chili. That was Plan B on the menu.

Robertia was less interested in a hearty meal than a comfy sleeping spot. One of those few vinyl couches was empty and she claimed it. As Robertia lay down someone asked, "Are you having fun?"

"Am I having fun?" she groggily repeated. "Sometimes."

"Has it been what you expected?"

"Yes," she said.

She gave last-minute instructions to her husband-handler for a wake-up call — they were still married and speaking. Seconds later, the only sound from the couch was a soft "zzz" as Robertia disappeared, head and all, into her sleeping bag.

While Robertia snoozed, William Kleedehn ventured into the night. This probably was going to be Kleedehn's last try for a championship. When Kleedehn left Pelly Crossing he was in the lead, but he was not alone on the trail for long. Jon Little was out there, too. So was Neff. After 300 miles (482 km) the trio seemed to have the strongest teams. The first of them to Dawson City would collect four ounces of gold.

If Neff won the gold, he would be out of excuses not to make his-and-her wedding rings and walk down the aisle with girlfriend, Tamra. Reynolds agreed that Neff's first idea of melting down the first gold into a ring was romantic, but when the idea stalled, she offered a suggestion. "Hugh, go to the store," she said.

Yep, despite the depressing economic climate, jewelers were still in business. Win more gold and the pressure would intensify on Neff to take action.

CHAPTER TEN

TWO KINDS OF ROOKIES

> "You know what it's like in
> the Yukon when it's 69 below;
> when the ice worms wriggle
> their purple heads through
> the crust of the pale blue snow."
> —Robert Service, *The Ballad of Blasphemous Bill*

1994 Those truly educated about dog-mushing history must have done a double take when they read the last name of a woman entered in the 1994 Quest. Nah, it couldn't be, they probably thought. But it was. Suzan Amundsen really was related to the famed Arctic and Antarctic explorer Roald Amundsen.

The Norwegian explorer, born in 1872, led the expedition that reached the South Pole first in 1911, thirty-five days ahead of Robert Scott's doomed group, and Amundsen was the first person to reach both the South and North Poles. He also led the first expedition to traverse the Northwest Passage. A monument in downtown Nome, Alaska, near the finish line of the Iditarod, commemorates Amundsen, who died in 1928 on a search for a missing friend.

Suzan Amundsen grew up in Penticton, British Columbia, but was living in Two Rivers, Alaska in 1993 raising two girls, when she first saw part of the Yukon Quest. The course practically ran through her yard.

"Oh, man, is that ever cool," she thought.

Amundsen had competed in some sprint races, but she became enchanted by long-distance mushing. She was forty-three, had no experience with winter camping, and took lessons from a neighbor before signing up for the Quest in 1994. "This is more for me," she said of racing through the backcountry. "I learned by doing it. I didn't have anybody to teach me. I like to camp and build a fire."

To prepare for the Quest, Amundsen trained at night, hiring a baby-sitter for her kids. She had the itch and was committed to the Quest, but she felt so much like a novice that she made out a will before the race. "I had my estate in order," she said. "There was a chance I might not come back."

It took Amundsen fifteen days, but she finished the Quest in twenty-first place. In all, she entered the Quest four times and the Iditarod twice, but it was incomparable leaving from Fairbanks and being out in the wild with her dogs in 1994. "The very first race you run, it's magic," she said.

Amundsen, a slender woman with long, brown hair who is now fifty-nine, thinks it was kind of strange that she fell in love with mushing at her age, but definitely believes her heritage accounts for it. "Genetically," she insists, "there is something to it. I just have the desire (to race)."

Genetically? That poses an interesting question. Roald Amundsen never had any children of record. Many people ask Suzan Amundsen about her last name and relationship to the famous explorer. She learned enough about Roald's exploits in the North to call herself a great-granddaughter descending from children he fathered out of wedlock with Eskimo women on the Northwest Passage trip between 1903 and 1906. Amundsen derives her connection to Roald from Ollie Amundsen, an Eskimo relative. "Everyone says they're my cousins," Suzan Amundsen said of Ollie Amundsen's clan.

Suzan has identified other relatives of Amundsen lineage, including a Scandinavian woman named Anna Issacson, who was a handler for past Iditarod champion Doug Swingley. They met in Nome, at the finish line of the Iditarod, just yards away from the monument of Roald Amundsen. Issacson approached Suzan and said, "I'm your cousin." It turned out that the women were living only about a mile apart in Two Rivers, Alaska. "That's unbelievable," Amundsen said.

However distant her connection to the explorer, Suzan Amundsen has no doubt that she has long-distance mushing in her blood.

━┼══

IN THE SAME 1994 race in which Amundsen made her debut, Lavon Barve was also a Quest rookie. Yet he was a grizzled veteran of the Iditarod. Barve came to the Quest to win, not merely to take part.

What Barve remembers best about his journey on the trail in the 1994 Yukon Quest was the cold, just how cold it was all the way between Fairbanks and Whitehorse. On a warm day it was minus 35 F (-37 C). The rest of the time it was minus 55 F (-48 C) or so. And it didn't bother him at all because he won.

Dog mushers always rave about the wilderness country they traverse, but Barve emphasized that he was mushing through God's country. He was more religious than almost all of the other competitors and eventually stepped away from the sport to become a missionary in Mexico.

When Barve made his entrance into the Quest, he was fifty years old and just three years shy of making that momentous decision to go south to do the Lord's work. But he was still viewed as a prime contender for long-distance mushing's biggest prizes.

A long-time veteran of the Iditarod, the Wasilla, Alaska print-shop owner, had an unusual mix of racing dogs in 1994. Some were old, a tad past their prime. Some of them were young, just coming into their own. Barve wore a thick mustache and had a thick body frame with wide shoulders. He was a strong man, but lighter weight mushers were beating him in the Iditarod. He dieted like a boxer trying to make weight, but he was a natural at 200 pounds (91 kilos). Barve's best finish was third in the Iditarod in 1990 and he decided to move his unorthodox, but mature team into the Quest for a year's experimentation.

"That one race, everything clicked for me," Barve said. "It was just a good race for me."

To veteran Quest racers, Barve was an unknown quantity. They knew him by reputation, but not trail habits. It was understood that he would be a contender, but no one knew if he would go out fast or try to finish fast. He had to be watched. Barve chose to start the race cautiously, content to hold back while others went out at a fast clip. "I remember one of the guys passed me," Barve said, "and he said, 'This is a dog race, get off your brake,' as he went by. I just decided I was going to go easy. I believe I was last into the first checkpoint. I always thought I was. I never really looked."

There is such a thing as playing possum in a long race and there is such a thing as digging yourself a hole. Barve said he went out slowly because of the cold conditions, his inexperience with the trail, and because of something he remembered past champion Dave Monson saying.

"Monson once said that there are two races in the Quest," Barve noted. "One to Dawson and one to Whitehorse. That kind of stuck in my head. I spent a lot of time trying to figure out how I'd run it. There was a map on the wall at the Quest checkpoints and I read it. In the end, I knew I would have to do what everybody else did based on the conditions, stopping where there was wood to build a fire."

There were thirty-eight mushers entered and Barve was in thirteenth place in Eagle. He started making up ground after that and when the teams hunkered down in Dawson City for their break, Barve was in sixth. He was satisfied with that position and was startled during the first night out of Dawson when he picked off those ahead of him one by one, or sometimes even two by two. "I pretty much caught them the first night and I wasn't prepared for that," Barve said.

Kathy Swenson, previously married to Iditarod champion Rick Swenson, was the first into Dawson, and became the first woman to earn the halfway gold prize. The other front-runners included Linda Forsberg, Jim Wilson, John Schandelmeier, and Peter Butteri.

Mushers were camped in small groups along the trail. Barve was surprised that he had eliminated their leads of up to six hours in a single day. Observers suggested that he was cutting rest, but he said that wasn't it at all, he was just sticking to his plan of running for four hours and resting for four hours. Once, he said, he mushed for five hours because he passed a couple of mushers and wanted to gain distance. Then he came upon another group of four mushers making camp.

"I just sort of went along with the gang," he said. "When I ran with them for a while I realized they were having to drop dogs from their teams. All of that speed at the beginning in the cold was making a difference."

Barve still had all fourteen dogs and would finish with thirteen. He liked how the strength of his team matched up against other contenders. At one point the mushers took a break, making camp at an old, battered cabin at McCabe Creek. The dilapidated cabin helped block the wind, but the wood had holes in it big enough to see through. After some rest, Barve had to go to the bathroom. There was no bathroom, so this meant trekking outside to take a leak and wrapping up in racing clothing for protection.

The other mushers thought he was going to leave, hit the trail, and build an advantage, so they all jumped up ready to mush, too. A chuckling Barve just went outside to take care of his business. It wasn't a bad strategy for disrupting the others' sleep, even though it was unintentional.

Barve was third into Carmacks behind Forsberg and Wilson, but not worried about his dog power. He remembers passing Wilson within a half-hour of leaving the town, then coming up on Forsberg, whom he thought was having difficulty controlling a leader. Forsberg actually rested her team with great caution, taking extra time when others pushed on. "There were good teams in there, as good as mine," Barve said, "but I had a strategy that I stuck with right from the start. I planned to let it rip at the end."

Especially given the extreme cold, Barve's approach was a sound, prudent one. The temperature kept dropping all of the way from Fairbanks to Dawson and that minus 55 F (-48 C) made an impression on Barve.

"I carried an extra rolled up parka for five years and never used it," he said of emergency equipment in his sled. "I took it out. It was minus 55 and the wind was blowing at my back."

—⊨—

"I WAS NEW TO THE RACE, but my advantage was that I had run the Iditarod a number of times. I had perfect gear, just all sorts of stuff to use to survive until you get to the next checkpoint."

Barve sweated a lot under his heavy gear, even in the frigid air, and he combated the threat of dehydration by constantly taking fluids. He had been slowed by dehydration in past races, but clued in to the need for frequent drinking.

"By the time I ran the Quest I was learning more about it," he said. "You don't want to see yourself out there at the checkpoint not being totally coherent. When I was inside a cabin I had to take off my outer clothes. If I got sweating badly, I got cold on the trail within an hour or hour and a half."

Halfway to Carmacks, Barve thought he might win. Near a cabin along the trail a little bit farther on, however, Barve reached a confusing spot. He did not see any trail markers. He continued on to a Y in the trail. There were trail markers on both sides. "You could go either way," he said. "But there was somebody pulling a sled and he went to the left, so that's how I went. I went for a long time again and didn't see any markers and then I came out on Lake Laberge. I didn't know if I was really on the trail, but I thought so because I had seen it sporadically."

Barve wanted to snack his dogs, but he was afraid to stop because he thought he would be passed. Mushing on the lake he used an ear plug to listen to a radio broadcast. He dozed off on his sled, and then woke abruptly when he heard his name mentioned.

"I hear something about Lavon Barve," he said. "That I was in the lead. I didn't know for sure before that."

The Y in the trail fooled him. "I had nobody to follow, no mark, no trail, no sled runners," Barve said.

At the far end of Lake Laberge, some 300 people waited to see the lead musher. The trail veered off and Barve never stopped to talk. Then Barve mushed on to the Whitehorse finish line alone, winning easily. His winning time of 10 days, 22 hours, 44 minutes was swift and about 2¾ hours ahead of second-place Wilson. Jim Wilson of Ambler, Alaska said the cold was intense. "I'm going to find a warm house and not leave it for a week," he said at the finish line.

Barve was both champion and rookie of the year, as well as the winner of $20,000. Although it is a victory he is proud of, he doesn't remember much fanfare on the Canadian side. When he got home to Wasilla, though, there was a large congratulatory sign erected near his house.

Barve did not race either the Quest or the Iditarod in 1995. He placed fourteenth in the Iditarod in 1996 and sixth in 1997, and then retired. At the Iditarod finish line in Nome, Barve announced that he was going to devote his life to the service of the Lord. Wearing a turquoise parka that on the back was scripted "Jesus Saves" and featured a large cross, Barve said he was going to sell his dog team.

Suffering from ulcers and other ailments that he did not specify, Barve described an increase in the intensity of his faith. He called himself "a lukewarm Christian for thirty-five years. Your worldly possessions don't mean much when the doctors talk about you might not be here." When he got sick, Barve said, others prayed for his health so devotedly that he was cured. "The Lord healed me — period," he said.

Although he had just pocketed $25,000 and completed his fastest Iditarod in 9 days, 21 hours and change, Barve planned to pay back the Lord with volunteer work for saving him. With those comments, Barve disappeared from the Quest and Iditarod. The public appearances he began making in Alaska and the Yukon were not at mushing forums, but at tent ministries. He and his wife Betty kept that up until the early 2000s. Then, the Barves took their work to rural, poverty-stricken areas of Mexico.

"I didn't consider myself a guy that the Lord would choose to go out as an evangelist, but he's the one that does the choosing and you just do the best job that you can," Barve said. "I think, 'Somebody else can play the guitar better than me' and do this and that better than me, but they ain't doing it. People that are a lot more qualified and learned, but I just go."

The ministry efforts in Mexico began small in 2003. Barve drove south, transporting a tent across the U.S. border, and was required to explain his intentions in some detail at customs. Once, it took three days before he was allowed across the international border. The Barves drove to the Sonora area. Each trip cost them thousands of dollars. Then a relative arranged things so they could leave the tent permanently and the Barves began flying to Mexico. When they arrived the tent was already set up. Ultimately, two tents were erected in different regions where there were few churches. The Barves flew in and stayed for a couple of weeks at a time, traveling by bus.

One of the biggest adjustments Barve made was accommodating the weather. He was used to minus-whatever and was asked to give testimony in a tent where in late morning it was 100 degrees F (38 C). Sometimes Barve spoke to 120 people at a time, sometimes 250. The number of people surprised him in areas that looked empty.

"It didn't look like there were more than a few thatched huts," he said. "Sometimes you would wonder, 'Where did they all come from?' We set up right next to a beach and that was nice. We went off into plantation places where the farmers sometimes grow stuff, and I don't know what they're growing and I don't ask any questions. You get a chance to tell people about Jesus. It's pretty awesome."

This was also somewhat tricky because Barve is not fluent in Spanish. He has learned a little bit of Spanish on each visit, jotting down a few words to add to his expanding vocabulary, but his repertoire is still only about fifty words. Translators help out.

"One-on-one ministry is pretty awesome," he said.

Passing his sixty-fifth birthday, Barve planned to slow down the pace of his Mexican trips, but not eliminate them. "They keep asking me when we're going to come down," Barve said.

From the moment Barve announced his retirement from racing in 1997, he did not mush again. He sold his dogs. But he scratches his itch for the sport by volunteering each March as a race judge for the Iditarod. "I would probably not be interested in going out again and sleeping in a snow pile and having the tent blow half over. I've been there," Barve said.

Yet, he has been to the finish line of the Yukon Quest first. "That time it just seemed to click for me and it was a real blessing," Barve said. And even if Lavon Barve never rides a sled on the Quest trail again he knows one thing: He's on the all-time list of champions.

CHAPTER ELEVEN

IRON WILL

"The trees had been stripped by a recent wind of their white covering of the frost,
and they seemed to lean toward each other, black and ominous, in the fading light.
A vast silence reigned over the land." — Jack London, *White Fang*

2009 — After the motorcycle accident, the only future William Kleedehn saw for himself in Germany was a desk job. And even if he had only one good leg, that was a discordant picture. He sought an outdoor life, in an outdoors the bigger the better. It was Canada that invited him in, and it was the Yukon he invited himself to.

While recuperating from the crash that changed his life, Kleedehn saw a newspaper item about the result of the 1978 Iditarod Trail Sled Dog Race. A guy named Dick Mackey had defeated a guy named Rick Swenson by one second in a 1,100-mile (1,770-km) race. Kleedehn remembers his father Ernst saying, "Jesus, what kind of guys are these?" — meaning, boy, those guys must be tough. Kleedehn thought so, too.

Kleedehn grew up as one of four children on a dairy farm near Hanover, Germany that also raised potatoes, grain, and sugar beets. His father was a strict taskmaster who worked Kleedehn, his two brothers, and sister hard. Kleedehn trained to be a mechanic. His taste of outdoor freedom was riding a motorcycle through the neighboring countryside. He was eighteen on the day when a car traveling at high speed with only one headlight crossed the center line and slammed into him on his bike.

The hit-and-run impact threw Kleedehn into a ditch, tore off his helmet, and crushed his left side. His left hand was severely injured, his left hip nearly disintegrated, and his leg was shattered. Pieces of bones mixed with blood and muscles and arteries were ripped asunder. In the dim light, Kleedehn crawled towards the center of the rural road where a motorist stopped and then called for an ambulance.

Appalled by the loss of blood, one doctor feared that Kleedehn might have suffered brain damage. The musher later joked that this explained why he took up racing dogs. Kleedehn's brain was no worse off than it had been, but he spent seven weeks in the hospital, underwent multiple surgeries, and had his left leg amputated below the knee.

Diligent police investigation found the driver, who had been drunk. Kleedehn received a $30,000 insurance settlement. But under Germany's workmen's compensation law Kleedehn's disability prevented him from working in a repair shop. That ended his plan to become a mechanic. Inspired by the Iditarod finish and disgusted by his circumstances, Kleedehn told his family he was headed for the wide-open spaces of Canada.

His parents had come over from Communist East Germany. They did not feel at home in West Germany and talked about immigrating to another nation. After two world wars, Kleedehn said, he did not have a large family. "Our family is very, very tiny," he said. "I have a couple of brothers, one sister, and one uncle that is living. That is all. I never saw my grandparents and there is no other family that I know of. So I was not leaving a traditional bigger family that most people have."

Kleedehn had company when he moved to Canada. He moved to Winnipeg, and his parents bought a chicken farm in Manitoba. For a time, Kleedehn and his wife operated a combination motel, restaurant, and gas station on the Trans-Canada Highway. The business was tourist-oriented and gave Kleedehn a lot of free time in the winter.

Soon enough, Kleedehn was a dog owner, and by the late 1980s, was entering middle-distance races such as the 400-mile (644-km)

John Beargrease Sled Dog Marathon in Minnesota. At the Northern Manitoba Trappers' Festival in The Pas, Kleedehn met highly regarded sled-maker Tim White, who also was an Iditarod musher. Still, Kleedehn thought of himself as a short-haul racer. "I thought that I am not the kind of guy who can handle the Yukon Quest or the Iditarod," he said. "I didn't think it would be my cup of tea. I figured these were only for professional mushers." White and another musher convinced him otherwise.

With an artificial leg, sled-dog racing was going to be harder for Kleedehn. Kleedehn, who now lives in Carcross, met his disability head-on. He named his kennel "Limp-A-Long." In his official 2009 Yukon Quest biography, the question, "How did this name develop?" is followed by a wry comment: "You'll know when you see me."

Kleedehn entered the 1990 Quest and he finished seventeenth in 13 days and 17 hours. His debut remains his favorite race because everything was new and exciting. The experience hooked him.

"I think about that race many times because I had not a clue what I was doing and no idea what kind of country I was headed into," Kleedehn said. "You are on the Yukon River and going down the Yukon River. It's a big river. It seemed like a formidable landscape to me. It's tough country. I started to admire those people who were living there and doing their job as trappers."

Coming upon cabins and wondering about the people who lived in them was memorable. Seeing the sunsets lasting forever and looking forward to the sunrises was pure pleasure. Being out in the big empty country was awe-inspiring.

"I was just a tourist traveling through their country," Kleedehn said. "For me, it was the biggest adventure of my life. I was thinking, 'This can't be true.' I was familiar with the Beargrease or 300-mile races and they were just one leg of this race. Every time you came around the bend, there was something new."

Before moving to Carmacks, Kleedehn made periodic forays into the Quest. He raced again in 1993 and 1998, and started moving up in the standings, advancing to the ranks of contender. He was less starry-eyed than he had been in his first Quest, and he started experiencing some of the good and bad of the trail. Kleedehn has gotten used to the idea that most years there is going to be a cold snap, and that it often will come in the Dawson City area. But he is one of those mushers impervious to cold while traveling. It is time spent in checkpoints that gets him.

"You only feel cold when you have to take off some of your clothing," Kleedehn said. "A couple of years ago I remember there was a bit of a breeze on the Yukon River, just a little bit, not far from Circle, and I had to snack the dogs. It was like 50 (F) below. I didn't have my best mittens. They had worn out and I had to use some other mittens. So my hands were a little bit chilled from the get-go. By the time I snacked the dogs I had trouble putting my mittens back on. I managed to get one on, but I couldn't get the other one — it was the right hand — back on. I noticed that within another thirty or fifty seconds, unless I got that frigging mitten on I was going to severely freeze my hand. It was stiff already. I didn't even care if the dogs ran away."

Damage can occur that fast.

The more familiar Kleedehn became with the trail and how to maximize speed, the more he also realized how difficult it was going to be for him to win the Quest. There would always be places where his left leg would hold him back. "There's no going around it," he said. "Running with the sled is impossible. It means hopping off the sled and running around a chunk of ice or a tree. I'm not fast enough."

Kleedehn handles sleep deprivation well and he has a very powerful upper body, with thick shoulders, arms, and fingers. "I have to somehow whip the sled around a tree so the runners and the stanchion stay in one piece," he said.

Mushers admire Kleedehn's perseverance. They understand that his leg is a handicap. Rick Mackey, the 1997 Quest champion, said Kleedehn is an impressive competitor.

"I'll tell you, he's one of the toughest men I know," Mackey said. "He's got a lot of heart, that guy. He's just tougher. He's not out there being babied because of his leg. The only thing I think he can't do really well is snowshoe because his ankle doesn't bend. He never complains about it or anything. I would like to see him win some day."

Kleedehn had a breakthrough in 2001 when he finished third. He was fifth in 2002 and runner-up in 2003. His 2004 race was a disaster, however. Kleedehn came into believing it was his turn to take the title. Mushing well approaching Eagle Summit near Mile 101 on the Steese Highway, Kleedehn fell and broke his leg. The bad one. He cracked a bone above his knee and scratched.

"I slipped on a little glacier," he said. "That year I had won a couple of races in record time. That team was so good. Nothing could hold them back. And here I break my frigging leg in that race."

Kleedehn did the Iditarod in 2008 for the experience, but has focused almost all of his long-distance racing attention on the Quest. He lives not far from the Quest trail and he has only thirty dogs in his kennel. Unlike some major mushing outfits his sponsorship is limited. He thinks big-time mushing has gone too corporate and he doesn't believe he is enough of a businessman to compete with the richest kennels. He works as a carpenter and rents cabins to tourists in the off-season instead of selling himself.

"You have to willfully promote yourself," Kleedehn said. "Maybe I could have done that, but I would have to work all of the time, non-stop, during the summer. My kennel is too small to have a team that is top-notch every year. I would have to breed more dogs and hire more handlers. You have to run your kennel like a business if you want to have a top team all the time. That would be a change in lifestyle for me. "

KLEEDEHN SAID HE EXPECTED to pull back from long-distance races soon. Before he got too old, he wanted to try some other outdoor adventures. His friend Thomas Tetz had done that, Hans Gatt was talking about it, and Kleedehn was mulling it.

It just might be, Kleedehn said, that the chance to win had passed him by. Yes, he wanted to become champion of the Quest at least as much as others wanted it for him. But as he got older he realized he didn't need a crown to validate his racing career.

"I'm not bad, but I don't win many races," Kleedehn said. "You know, winning the Quest is only a psychological thing because other people think that if you won the race, then that counts for more. The attitude is the Olympic medal, gold, silver, bronze, everybody tries to win. Some people go to desperate measures. I say to myself, 'Hey, in ten years, who will remember who won that race?' Some local people, maybe, and some fans that are close to it, and the people who do it, but nobody else really cares. Fifty or a hundred years later, who gives a heck? I was thinking that for me, the most important thing has to be actually doing what I like to do. That's important."

And then in the 2009 race, Kleedehn found himself in the lead.

CHAPTER TWELVE

NO DISGRACE TO BE LAST

"We'll leave the light on for you." — Tom Bodett, Motel 6 commercial

1985-2008 Just inside the door at the Yukon Quest race headquarters at the end of Main Street in Whitehorse stands a large glass case. Inside the case stands a tall trophy with a wooden base with the names of last-place finishers inscribed on gold backing. The trophy is an over-sized replica of the red lantern.

The red lantern is awarded each year to the musher who is the last to cross the finish line. Those who scratch, drop out, quit, or are disqualified are not finishers and not eligible for the red lantern. Only those who complete the race can earn the award. And earn it they do. If the cynical wish to call the red lantern the booby prize, so be it, though a more polite term might be consolation prize. Still, anyone who mushes a dog team 1,000 miles (1,609 km) is deserving of respect. They will not receive a cash reward for a high placing, but the red lantern offers a specific type of respect for perseverance.

The red lantern signals that back-of-the-pack racers are not forgotten. Simply put, the red lantern is a symbol for those still out on the trail that a light has been left burning to guide them home.

Each year the last-place Quest finisher is given a replica of the trophy red lantern in the glass case. If any musher has set out to win the red lantern at the start of a race that is unknown. It's actually not easy to finish last because a musher has no idea how many of those ahead of him or trailing him might have dog difficulties or trail disasters that necessitate slowing way down. While winners of the Quest gain fame, the red lantern winners remain pretty much anonymous once they are handed the trophy. Race fans cannot easily name the last-place finisher in a given year, or even in the most recent year. While names are inscribed on that trophy in Whitehorse, otherwise the red lantern winners are obscured by time.

In some ways, Fairbanks journalist Brian O'Donoghue may be the most famous red lantern winner in Quest history. That's because he wrote a book called *Honest Dogs* about his only time on the trail in the 1998 race. O'Donoghue also wrote a book titled *My Lead Dog Was a Lesbian* about his year racing the Iditarod. As it so happened, O'Donoghue ended up with the distinction, neither planned nor sought, of finishing last in both races. He has a bookend set of red lanterns. For some time, when he appeared at bookstore signings, O'Donoghue brought a suitcase. He threw open the satchel on a table and withdrew his red lanterns, brought along as eye-catching props.

Years later, O'Donoghue's red lanterns have been dinged up a little bit in moves, but they have a place of honor on the mantle above the fireplace in his home.

"They were exiled to the garage for a little bit," O'Donoghue said. "Now they're in the house. The last time they saw the public I took them to an elementary school in Two Rivers. A guy who runs a bed and breakfast tried to buy one of my red lanterns. I said, like, 'No, you don't do that.' Then he said how about if he built a case and put it in there, but I thought I would never get it back. You have to hold on to them. I read about people who lose their Super Bowl rings. The idea that you would hock something like that, I don't think so."

That story indicates there is some cache to owning a red lantern. However, mushers themselves who have won the red lantern seem to have mixed feelings about them. They entered the Quest trying to do their best and if they did not believe that they could win the race they definitely figured to finish better than last.

Wayne Hall of Eagle finished twenty-sixth, and last, in 2002. He said he does not own a large home and there really isn't a good place to display his red lantern. So it is kind of out of sight, if not out of mind. The red lantern lives behind a bookshelf. It was a surprise to Hall when he realized he was going to finish last. For quite a while, for many miles, that's not how his race was unfolding.

"At one point, there were thirteen people behind me," Hall said. "Then I saw the standings and it was, 'Where are they all at?' I was pretty bummed about it." He was happy that he finished with all of the fourteen dogs he started with, though. "I finished with class," Hall said.

The red lantern winner in 1992 was George Cook, who came from New Hampshire to train for and race in the Quest and whose wife Ann Mariah Cook wrote a book about his Quest. Cook's biggest reward was finishing and his wife does not make a big deal in the book about his receiving the red lantern. She calls it "the type that hangs from a train's caboose." Cook's payoff was at the finish line when his daughter hugged him, and his family shouted out, "We did it!"

At the start of the 2000 Quest, Deborah Bicknell, fifty-four, of Juneau, Alaska, joked around about needing Geritol boosts to keep her aging body going on the trail. She survived, doing just well enough to capture the red lantern in twenty-first place, almost five days behind the winner.

An oddity occurred during the 2005 race. Blake Freking placed well in twelfth, but also was last. It was a small field with a number of dropouts. Freking even collected $2,500 in prize money. In 2006, there were twenty-two starters, but only eleven finishers and last place was Regina Wycoff, who won $2,900. A much happier Wayne Hall was tenth that year and collected $3,300.

Yukon musher Kyla Boiven won the red lantern in 2008. But her finish was solid. In fifteenth place, in the twenty-fifth and richest Quest, she won $4,000 in prize money. The placing gnawed at her, but she admitted that finishing last was better than not finishing at all. "It's cooler to get the red lantern," Boiven said. "The red lantern is a prize."

Boiven did not realize she was in last place. Mushing into Central on the Alaska side, she was given the word by checkers. "What happened?" she asked. Others behind her had dropped out. "So it's not really last. Maybe I'm not a competitive team. I love running the race. I love being on the trail. I love running the dogs."

The red lantern is sponsored by the White Pass & Yukon Route, the railroad that once offered service between the Yukon and Alaska, but now operates only locally in the Yukon for tourists in the summer. For the anniversary 2008 race, a special red lantern was made. Boiven's prize is more utilitarian than O'Donoghue's or Hall's commemorative red lantern.

"It was specially made," Boiven said. Her red lantern came with a light-sensitive gizmo. "It turns itself on. It's my night light," Boiven said.

O'Donoghue finished last in Bruce Lee's victory race. Lee's winning time was 11 days, 11 hours, 27 minutes. O'Donoghue's last-place time was 16 days, 8 minutes. Even if O'Donoghue did not believe he was capable of winning, he did think he would be closer to the front.

Having the book among his achievements means that O'Donoghue is also better remembered as a red lantern winner than most. "It sticks in some respects," he said. "In a conversation where there is talk about the race someone says, 'Oh,' when I say I did the Quest. But I almost feel compelled to tell them, 'Well, I finished last.' It's kind of like a disclaimer." But they usually say, 'You finished.' I don't mind having finished last. In that race, in particular, it was a little nip and tuck that I would finish at all. I finished with only seven dogs."

O'Donoghue misjudged the weather on a run early in the race. Mushing in the heat of the day took a toll on the team and the warmth slowed the dogs down and led to some of them being dropped. He also got confused on parts of the trail.

"The Quest is very, very historic and you feel that every step of the way, just about," he said. "But you are running through country that for the most part is very sparsely traveled these days.

So it has less base to the trail and it's easier to lose if it gets blown in. Sections of the Yukon River, the jumbo ice section from one year to the next, can be insane. It can pile up with these blocks of ice. It's going through country that's hard traveling."

As someone who has been last in both the Iditarod and Quest, O'Donoghue has a rare perspective. The Iditarod, called "The Last Great Race on Earth," is harder because the competition from more mushers is relentless, he believes. The Quest, called "The Last Great Adventure," is harder because of the terrain, he thinks. "The failure rate, percentage-wise, is historically higher in the Quest. I think that's because the trail itself bums out the dogs. You're starting with fewer dogs and you are more on your own on the trail."

O'Donoghue kept talking to himself in the Quest, trying to convince himself that he could catch mushers he was chasing. But he was carrying a GPS unit and when he measured his speed he got a reading of 7.1 mph (11.4 kph). When he measured the speed of others he was going after he got a reading of 10 mph (16 kph). The math was disheartening. Once, leaving a checkpoint, he jokingly announced that his team was charging ahead "with blinding speed."

He had a whale of a time getting over 3,450-foot (1,052-meter) American Summit, endured a dog rebellion on 3,685-foot (1,123-meter) Eagle Summit when the dogs essentially looked up and barked, "You want us to go there?" And he overslept in a warm trail cabin.

O'Donoghue said he spent a long time analyzing his results in the Iditarod and in the Quest, examining how he had finished last in both. In the Iditarod, he said he felt he should have finished higher, but in the Quest, given the mistakes he made early that reduced his team, he felt fortunate to make it to the end.

"You kind of think you've let your dogs down a little bit," O'Donoghue said. "Anything can happen. Just getting over Eagle Summit, I had a really hard time. I lost a lot of time at Mile 101 just because I was physically rummy and shot after Eagle Summit. I mean, I'm not a great athlete."

Crowds gather when the winner of the Quest shows up in Fairbanks or Whitehorse. Because the Quest is a round-the-clock event, however, depending on the time of day the crowd may be smaller as other mushers finish. People might not want to climb out of bed at 3 a.m. in the cold to see even the second-place musher. Occasionally, the red lantern musher gets more attention.

"I've talked to other folks that have talked about how disappointing it is to get to the finish line when virtually nobody is there," O'Donoghue said. "I have made it a point to go out and see other red lantern winners come in. There are usually people there. It's a little bit like, 'Hey, guy, go for it,' in the cheering for that guy."

Call it a tribute in applause and huzzahs for the underdog. And then the lovely parting gift of the red lantern is presented.

YUKON QUEST PHOTO GALLERY

PHOTOS BY LEW FREEDMAN

▲ There was a big crowd in Whitehorse in February, 2009 as mushers left at three-minute intervals to start the long, cold run to Fairbanks.

▲ Four-time Quest champion Lance Mackey, known for the affection he shows his dogs, said bonding with the huskies helped him overcome throat cancer.

▶Martin Buser of Big Lake, Alaska, had won the Iditarod Trail Sled Dog Race four times, but was a rookie when he entered the Quest in 2009.

▲ Dog care is a priority. The dogs are checked often by veterinarians. Dr. Kathleen McGill of Columbus, Ohio, was the chief veterinarian in the 2009 race.

▶It's snack time as Yukon musher Michelle Phillips rummages through her dog food drop at the Central Checkpoint.

▲ Sonny Lindner of Two Rivers, Alaska, won the first Quest in 1984 when organizers weren't sure the race could be completed. Lindner continued to race dogs into his sixties.

▶Frank Turner is the old man of the Quest, having raced twenty-four times. Turner maintains a kennel on the outskirts of Whitehorse.

▲ Former Illinois resident Hugh Neff first ran the Quest on a shoestring budget. He became a top contender who, but for one serious error, might have become a champion.

▶ The huskies hang out in boxes in their mushers' dog trucks before the start, and rest on straw beds at the checkpoints.

◀Sebastian Schnuelle of Whitehorse wore a husky hat at the start of the 2009 race. He was still smiling in Fairbanks, below, as he scored a surprise come-from-behind win.

▲ Bill Cotter of Nenana, Alaska, a past Yukon Quest champion, relaxes by his dog truck in Dawson City in 2009 after completing a companion race.

▲ Rookie Newton Marshall of Jamaica acquitted himself well in the 2009 event, finishing thirteenth, but often expressed how cold he was.

▲ William Kleedehn, a transplanted German living in the Yukon, has run the race twelve times and is a favorite of fans because he races with one artificial leg.

◀ Jon Little of Kenai Peninsula, Alaska, shown leaving Dawson City, remained near the front of the pack in the 2009 quest, finishing third.

▶Vern Halter won the 1990 Quest. Retired from competition, Halter runs a tourist business in Willow, Alaska.

▶▶Brian O'Donoghue of Fairbanks won the red lantern in the 1998 Quest. He is the only musher ever to have finished last in both the Quest and the Iditarod race.

CHAPTER THIRTEEN

A CANADIAN TRIUMPH

"He was a sturdy traveler, and his wolf-dog could work harder and travel farther on less grub than any other team in the Yukon." – Jack London, *The Sea Wolf*

1995 Frank Turner probably has mushed more miles in the Yukon Territory than anyone still running the trails. His dogs, pampered by some standards, and well fed by the pickiest nutritionist's demands, are so well cared for that Turner's fastidiousness has earned him the nickname "Grandma."

He is past sixty now, hair still mostly brown, but his beard shows a mixing of brown and gray. The man also known as "Rabbi" for his Jewish heritage remains a living, breathing, active link to the origins of the Quest in 1984. Turner raced in twenty-four of the first twenty-six Quest events, winning the championship in 1995.

Those who know Turner tease him because he talks a lot. He's a veritable warehouse of historical knowledge. They also tease him about his height. "I say I'm five-foot-six — in bunny boots," Turner chuckles. For those not in the know, bunny boots are the thick, rubber-soled footwear of choice in the North. They keep feet warm and happen to add two inches to one's height.

Turner and his wife, Anne, live on the outskirts of Whitehorse. He has a palatial dog yard off the highway, where 127 huskies live, train, and pull sleds for tourists who come from all over the world to experience the Yukon backcountry. Turner's dogs carry visitors into the snowy woods, far removed from the noise and bustle of civilization — a memorable experience. The active dogs live in wooden box houses. Those who are retired or ill sleep in an equipment shed. The kennel is so large that Turner has marked the dogs' neighborhoods with street signs. A dog might reside at the intersection of "Quest" and "Dawson" streets.

Ten-year-old Kirby hangs out inside. After running six Yukon Quests with Turner, he deserves the plusher accommodations, lying on a blanket and removed from the cold. Another Turner favorite, Decaf, twelve years old and a veteran of seven Quest runs, is dying of cancer and spends much of his time indoors, too.

After reluctantly coming north with a friend in 1973, Turner was struck by the Yukon's romance and remoteness. He became a permanent resident in 1974, squatting on some land with his first dog, Skookum, and since has become the elder statesman of Yukon mushing.

Turner never had a tree fort as a kid, but soon he was living in an approximation of one. He built a tiny cabin from discarded wood he'd scrounged from along the Alaska Highway. His bed, scavenged from the brush, was suspended halfway up the wall. Turner called his new home "the hovel." He describes the cabin roof as 'kind of concave." Rain or snow melted through a leak in the roof, and Turner hung a string at the spot, so the drip went directly down into a bucket.

Turner acquired a second dog, Chimo, and third, Chico, who gave him a litter of five puppies. He found a sled so old that he described it as "an historical artifact." With puppies and a sled, Turner did the only thing that made sense. "That's when I went and got a book about how to make harnesses by hand," he said. When the puppies were a bit older, he hooked them to the sled and mushed a short distance to nearby McLean Lake to haul water. That was the beginning.

Friends bugged Turner to enter a local race called the Yukon Sourdough Rendezvous, but he resisted. When he was in high school, Turner had dabbled in a variety of sports, and said he was a poor loser, so he wasn't attracted to dog-sled races. He didn't want to spoil the wonder of the experience of driving his dogs in the backcountry, enjoying the scenery. But the rendezvous was the centerpiece of the local winter carnival, and finally, with a what-the-heck attitude, Turner entered.

He was surprised at what a good time he had even though he didn't have a top finish. In fact, he didn't really care how well he finished at all. He was still having the same kind of fun riding the runners behind his dogs. Turner entered more races and enjoyed them. All of this pre-dated the Quest. The sprint-race distances were perhaps 12 miles (19 km) in a day.

The racing taught Turner about himself. He realized that he was a kinder and gentler person in his twenties than when he had been a hard-core competitive athlete in high school. With maturity, Turner recognized that it was him, the human, and not the dogs, making the mistakes in races and costing the team better finishes. He embraced new ideas.

"I started changing my approach to things and was not being so reliant on the way things had been done," he said. "It didn't mean that was necessarily the best way to do it." People seemed to be growing more sensitive to the feelings of animals in the late 1970s and early 1980s, too, whether they were dogs, horses, or some other beast. "It's also my belief that women had a profound effect in mushing," Turner said. "They didn't buy into the macho way of dealing with teams and competition. You had people that talked to their dogs like little kids. The dogs would eat it up. A dog team, really, is about relationships. I think the mushers that are most consistently successful are the ones that build the strongest relationships with their dogs."

Turner became an active sprint musher, recorded better finishes, yet found he was strangely dissatisfied at the end of the race. "You'd go 10 or 12 miles (16-19 km) as fast as you could, then you put the dogs away and waited for the next day," he said.

Turner extended his racing by competing in the 200-mile (322-km) Percy de Wolfe middle-distance event, but when he heard about a new marathon race between Whitehorse and Fairbanks, he became excited. He attended the first organizational meetings on the Canadian side. "It was longer and that's what I was looking for," Turner said.

When the mushers gathered at the starting line for the first Yukon Quest on February 25, 1984, Turner was there, twelve dogs in harness and driving a sled that weighed probably 50 pounds (23 kilos) instead of the more streamlined, half-the-weight variety used today. He could not have imagined how much the race would define his life. Racing in the event every year, training for it, making a living offering tourist dog sled trips to see the same beautiful country, Turner was on his way to becoming Canada's most famous musher.

In the beginning, sleds were built like tanks, prepared for all kinds of collisions on all type of terrain. The makeup of the route was unknown and it was best to be prepared for rugged territory. "That's what made it really exciting," Turner said of the unknown factor. "The first time we had no idea what the heck we were getting into and it was just absolutely great."

Community support was strong, mushers bunked on church pews in small villages, and those who owned cabins on the trail threw open their doors. "The people were glad to see us," Turner noted. "Instead of being a closed community where hardly anybody came, now people were coming. They would sometimes cook bread for you, or have a stew, and (had) a place where you could pull your dogs off the river and get a little bit of rest, or relief from the wind and cold," Turner said. Mushers and their big race were coming to town and it meant something during a long winter. The Quest eliminated cabin fever for a little while. "People were coming with dog teams and it appealed to that frontier spirit and everybody identified with it," Turner said. Even summer residents who locked up their cabins for the season hopped on snowmachines and opened their cabins for the race.

A few years into the race, one schemer tried to change one cabin's dynamic that previously had been a welcome spot for mushers. He announced he was going to charge $20 for mushers to park their dogs, "Some guy's trying to set up his idea of a bed and breakfast," Turner said. "We're in the middle of a race. It was just terrible. There was just about a riot out there." The plan to make money disintegrated quickly.

It took more than 13 days and 20 hours, but Turner reached the finish line in fourteenth place, surprised that he actually won $600. Just behind him, by one minute, was Wilson Sam of Huslia, Alaska, who partnered with Turner for long distances on the trail.

Sam's wife, Lorena, had urged him to pack his sled heavily for the great unknown. Turner loaded up on protein bars and nutritional snacks that did nothing for his palate. Sam carried bannock and traditional Native foods. Turner, perhaps the smallest man on the course, and Sam, who stood about six-foot-three, shared meals. "I would get smoked salmon from him and I'd give him these protein bars," Turner said. "He loved the bars and I loved the fish. We were kind of an odd couple because he was so much taller than I."

Lorena Sam cajoled her husband into taking a tent with him, too, and he slept in it when he and Turner camped along the Yukon River. But he didn't like it. He called Lorena and told her he had used it, as per her wishes, but he wasn't going to keep carrying it. He had enough stuff in his sled. She was not thrilled by his choice.

The mushers stayed together heading into the final 100 miles (161 km), then came to windswept Lake Laberge. It was all ice and no trail markers. Sam looked at Turner and said, "Okay, this is your country, which way do we go?" Turner didn't have the slightest idea. He led them up the wrong slough and they had to double back. Then they dropped to their knees trying to discern paw prints from dogs that had previously passed.

Somehow they managed. Earlier in the race, outside of Dawson, Turner had broken his glasses. Although he told Sam he didn't have to wait for him, the Alaskan waited four hours while they were fixed, saying, "No, we're doing this together." He suggested they sprint to the finish line at the end of the race if they were still together. As they approached Whitehorse, the men stopped their teams side by side. There was only about 100 yards (91 meters) or so to go, and the spectators wondered what the heck they were doing. A friend of Turner's walked up and Turner asked him to count backwards from ten. They sprinted for the finish and Turner's leaders cut off Sam's leaders, and Turner beat his friend to the line.

"It was just a really fantastic experience for me to be with him," Turner said. "He's such a fine, fine person."

After his first race, the Quest became a habit for Turner. He got better and faster at it too. Once, in a casual nod to his background, Turner rewarded his dogs with kosher salami at the finish line. "I wanted them to have the best," Turner said.

Turner placed sixteenth in 1985, twelfth in 1988, tenth in 1989 and 1993, but was coming off a scratch in 1994. Turner ran into some bad luck at Eagle Summit that year. His dogs misjudged the trail, staying straight when they needed to make a sharp left. Their paws started breaking through the crust of snow and they began heading downhill in the wrong direction. "There was no trail and I knew we had made a serious mistake. I turned around and tried to get off the hill, but the snow underneath the crust was like sugar, a granular kind of snow. You just kept on wading into it just like it was quicksand. I was getting exhausted. It was late at night, dark, and the wind was really, really blowing. I ended up spending eleven hours there."

Kathy Swenson came over the summit and saw Turner's headlamp in the distance. She began to mush in his direction, but he warned her to stop. She parked her dogs and walked over to Turner. "What happened to you?" she asked. "What do you mean, what happened to me?" Turner replied. "Your face," she said. In his battle to extricate the dogs, Turner had frostbitten his face and hands. Turner escaped his trap by mushing downhill and making a big circle. It cost him time, but he regained the trail. He did not regain his equilibrium.

"After Eagle Summit, I never really stopped shivering inside my parka," Turner said. He dropped out.

Mistakes come dear on the Quest trail, but in 1995, Turner made up for his hard-won education and disappointments. Turner never planned to become a regular in the Quest, but he loved it and worked hard improving and gaining knowledge.

"It cost me my first marriage," he said. "It came down to me being forced to make a decision, and that's not a good position to be in." On the other hand, the first wife is history and Turner still has a kennel full of dogs, so we know how it turned out. As Turner lined up for the start of the 1995 Quest in Whitehorse, he never had placed in the top five and never had collected major prize money in the race. Still, he had a large following among local mushers and fans for running the race every year. He was a symbol of local pride and that appreciation mushroomed when he won the race. Given his humble beginnings in the Quest and his shortage of competitive fire, Turner said, "I was one of the most unlikely people to have won that race."

LARRY "COWBOY" Smith was a brash, wise-cracking race veteran with a loud sense of humor who liked to set a fast pace in his races. Although he almost always burned out, Smith believed that one day he would win either the Quest or the Iditarod with his dogs by setting a scorching pace that no one could keep up with. He tantalized spectators for years.

Smith's approach was typical in the 1995 Quest. He darted for the lead out of Whitehorse and was first into Carmacks 140 miles (225 km) down the trail. He blasted into Dawson City first and claimed the halfway gold prize. But by then it was apparent that this was going to be a special year for Turner. He took a longer rest and was sixth into Dawson, but he notched the fastest time between Carmacks and the halfway point. "These guys are just beautiful," Turner said of his dogs before he took his required rest break.

By Eagle, Jim Wilson had clawed out a small lead. A handful of dog drivers, including Turner, stopped to rest at the checkpoint, but Smith chose to mush on through. The cautious choice proved wiser. In the latter stages of the race in Alaska, Turner's well-rested dogs were the strongest. In Angel Creek, Turner's team was aching to run. Wilson said that Turner's approach was sound. "He's been babying his team and they're moving right along now."

He wasn't the only one who acknowledged the superiority of Turner's dogs. "It's over for first place," said musher Jay Cadzow.

It was around 3 a.m., the middle of the night, with a temperature hovering near minus 20 F (28 C), when Turner's team, guided by leaders Grizzly and Hooligan, mushed over the frozen Chena River into downtown Fairbanks. American and Canadian flags fluttered in the night. Turner, then forty-seven, collected $15,000 and set a race record of 10 days, 16 hours, 18 minutes. Former champion Joe Runyan said Turner deserved praise for having the guts to stick to his own race plan regardless of what other mushers were doing.

"I can't believe I won this race," Turner said. Wilson finished second, forty-nine minutes behind, and Jay Cadzow was third, another half-hour behind Wilson. Cor Guimond made it four mushers across the finish line in less than eleven days — a very fast pace.

Frank Turner's victory was one of the race's turning points, said John Firth, the former president of the Quest's Canadian board of directors. A victory by a local musher was a big deal in the Yukon, and Turner attracted unprecedented media attention across Canada. After the triumph, Turner took his lead dogs on a national morning TV show and, as Turner earnestly described his race, a dog sat on a guest couch, in full view, licking its testicles. The riotous reaction imbedded the scene in the national consciousness and boosted the profile of the Quest.

"People in the Yukon identified very strongly with Frank," Firth said. "The timing was perfect. It was probably the most pivotal year we've ever had."

Turner's win was recorded a year after Bruce Johnson's death during a training run. Johnson always had been supportive of his friend, often encouraging him to let out more of his competitive instincts. Turner thought about Johnson frequently during the race, particularly as he mushed along the Chena River on the frosty night, closing in on the finish line.

"I feel kind of strange sometimes telling this story," Turner said. "But I had the sense that Bruce was really nearby. He used to make fun of me when I was losing and now he was making jokes because I was going to win. I was laughing. I clearly remember the experience of laughing and it made me feel so good because I could almost hear the tone of his voice and that he was so close. It was a special kind of feeling. I don't try to explain this at all, but it was a special moment."

From a distance, others may attribute such a sensation to fatigue and hallucinations, but Turner doesn't over-analyze the moment and just accepts that it was Johnson's voice in the background in a mystical sense as he mushed to the championship.

Winning the Quest in 1995 constitutes a proud entry on Turner's list of accomplishments. It changed his life, he said, because the world loves winners more than losers and he went from being known regionally to known nationally. He said he also learned lessons worth remembering in that race and how challenges reveal character. It is easy to stay in a good mood when things are going well, but how you respond when things go wrong is telling.

"I learned, most importantly, that you've got to believe in yourself, and you've got to believe in your team absolutely," Turner said, adding, "How we are in this most difficult situation is what defines us."

The win helped make Turner more of a public figure. Fans came out of the woodwork. They recognized him, patted him on the back, and, in his mind, put more pressure on him. As the 1996 race approached, Turner felt the heat. "I would have First Nations elders come up to me and say, 'Frank we're going to pray for you,'" Turner said. "'Frank, we're going to pray that you win the Quest again.' In the next race I was really struggling and the thoughts of those expectations were like a weight around my ankles, like a ball and chain."

Turner tried to summon back the encouragement of Johnson, tried to hear his friend's guidance just as he had the year before. "I couldn't make that happen," Turner said. "I was trying to will something back that I didn't understand, and make it come back to bail me out the second year. I realized that whatever was going to happen, I was going to have to do it myself." Another friend and racer, John Anderson, provided solace and good advice. "People were wishing me well, but the most important thing said to me was from John when he said, 'Frank, never stop believing in your team.' That became my mantra through the second half of the race."

John Schandelmeier dominated the 1996 race, claiming his second win, but Turner finished a solid fifth, and was pleased about the way he had rallied and handled adversity.

"There seem to be some universal sports principles where all of us go a lot farther when we believe in ourselves," he said. "It's the doubts that hold us all back and it's how we manage those doubts. If you have had a commitment to preparation and training, that allows you to do your best. I'm not trying to go out there and beat somebody else. I'm going out there not to beat myself and to be the best I can be."

Turner finished second in 1997, fifth in 1998, third in 2000, sixth in 2001, and fifth in 2004. Although Turner never won the Quest again, he vaulted from nowhere to the championship in one year and maintained his status as a contender for years. The belief in his own ability — and his dogs' — lingered and provided a permanent level of confidence following the 1995 victory.

"You've got something that a lot of other people are trying to get and the experience and memories of what it was that got you there in the first place," Turner said. "A lot of people are trying to figure it out, but you've got concrete experience (of what it takes to win). You've got to remember what got you there and hang on to the things that are important."

Turner competed in the twenty-fifth annual Quest in 2008. He entered the 2009 race, but had to withdraw because of a separated shoulder that required surgery. Turning sixty-two in the summer of 2009 made him think he might retire from Quest competition, but he knew better than to say never again.

Nor did Turner abandon the trail. With the 127 dogs in his kennel used to offer tourist trips to people from all over the world, Turner is still exploring the terrain he loves. One of those visitors from Canada or Europe might get the Yukon Quest bug and ask Turner to train him. He could see that happening. Turner might yet become a Quest coach.

CHAPTER FOURTEEN

TRAIL BREAK

"A good sleep does wonders for a musher's confidence." — John Firth, *Yukon Quest*

1995 Hugh Neff was forthright, as he usually is. "I love Dawson City," he said.

The sun was bright and the temperature was minus 15 F (-26 C) as dog-handlers and mushing fans mingled at the Dawson City Visitors Centre on Front Street, waiting for the mushers to arrive with their fourteen-dog teams halfway through the 2009 Yukon Quest. The thing on most minds was an intermission. With a mandatory break and the freedom under the rules to allow handlers to do most of the work with the team, instead of taking care of all of the chores themselves, mushers could relax and sleep in real beds with pillows and other fancy accoutrements such as blankets and sheets.

Sleep was not what Neff thought about first as he stood at the checkpoint as the clock ticked towards midnight. "I've got to get to the bar at The Pit before it closes," he said.

Fans ate at the Jack London Grill, one of the few businesses open in winter. Dawson City is geared to pleasing summer tourists, not gold-rush prospectors. Many buildings are purple, red, and yellow — more adorable than grizzled.

A few hotels accommodated the Quest crowd, including the notorious Bombay Peggy's, decorated as the nineteenth century brothel it was. Musher Martin Buser and his wife were assigned The Lipstick Room. Whatever happens in Dawson City, stays in Dawson City.

ABOUT TWO MILES from the Visitors Centre where the humans gathered, a special area was staked out for the dogs. The provincial park, which in summer rents numbered camping spaces, was the designated doggie camp. Each musher had his own space in trees where tents were erected, fires built, and beds of straw were laid out for the huskies. Some handlers posted welcome signs. It was quite the cozy environment for the dogs, as several humans waited on them. They may not have been interested in beer like Neff, but the dogs were served the most nutritious eats and drinks mushers could afford.

The Quest has strict rules banning outside assistance during the race, but Dawson City is the one exception. Handlers assume dog care as mushers rest and recuperate.

Racers leave Whitehorse at three-minute intervals and Dawson City is where the time is evened out and factored into departures for the second half of the race. The midway point offers time for sleep and reflection on one's place in the race and time to contemplate race strategy. Neff decided he was going to jettison his Johnny Cash T-shirt as a bottom layer and replace it with a "Yes We Can" Barack Obama T-shirt. Perhaps the attire would be a difference maker.

There is no mushing fan of the year competition, but Frank Hauze, fifty-five, of Hazelton, Pennsylvania, earned a doff of the fur hat. A retired long-haul truck driver who had followed mushing on the Internet for several years, Hauze was on the trip of a lifetime, following the Quest and the Iditarod. He grew friendly with Jim and Nancy Davis, two of Buser's handlers, and obtained some souvenir booties. "I always liked Martin Buser because he was a gentleman," Hauze said. "He seemed like he would have the time of day for you. It absolutely turned out to be true."

The claimant to the halfway prize of four ounces of gold was a surprise. Jon Little was reported to be leading, but just outside of Dawson, William Kleedehn passed him with his headlamp burned out. Kleedehn said he thought he was passing a recreational team.

Little was wistful about losing the halfway prize. "I would have loved to give my wife some gold," he said.

Previously unknown mishaps came to light. Fairbanks musher Brent Sass told people one of his dogs ran into a tree heading into Carmacks. He was running three dogs in his team named after characters in the bowling movie "The Big Lebowski," a modern comedy classic. The dog apparently did not pick up the 7-10 split.

Buser said he had made beginner's mistakes in falling to ninth place. Going out too fast, he was forced to drop four dogs and felt he lost his chance to win. He didn't bring enough food on the 201-mile (323-km) run from Pelly Crossing, was reduced to eating a single piece of candy when he ran low on food, and didn't put on his warmest parka when he got cold.

"I felt bad for my guys (dogs) that I couldn't give them as much as they wanted," Buser said. "That's just being a rookie. I went too fast. I got too carried away. I was like a dumb rookie. It was just stupid."

Jamaican Newton Marshall arrived in one piece. He was still a surf-and-sand guy, but after spending parts of the preceding two winters living in the Yukon hanging out with Hans Gatt, Marshall had accumulated his share of merit badges. Marshall wore a jacket that across the back read, "Mush Mon."

Some mushers crashed immediately after checking in. Others were too hyper to sleep. Being in the middle of a race where they had to be hyper-vigilant about the weather, their dogs, and taking care of things, they couldn't slow their brains down so swiftly. They chit-chatted, drank beer, downed chili, coffee or hot chocolate.

Rookie Josh Cadzow slept thirteen hours, a possible Quest record, but when he tried to leave the checkpoint, his dogs refused to move and he scratched. Sebastian Schnuelle also slept well and announced upon rising, "I'm brand new."

William Kleedehn buzzed around the Visitors Centre. His old friend Thomas Tetz predicted that Kleedehn was poised to do well, but needed to calm down. "The tougher it gets, the better," Tetz said, but added: "He talks a little too much and should sleep more."

Every musher, regardless of goal, leaves the starting line with a certain amount of optimism. Jason Mackey, new to the Quest, and seeking to represent the family name well, set out for Fairbanks trying to follow the game plan spelled out by his champion brother Lance. Instead, Mackey had just about the worst luck of anyone racing. Jason had trouble finding the Scroggie Creek dog drop, had to cope with dogs battling an intestinal virus, and had to sweet-talk dogs that didn't seem to want to run hard. "From day one, it's just been unbelievable," he said. Mackey's dreams went up in smoke, and he scratched.

So did Dave Dalton, the friendly, twenty-year mushing veteran from Healy. Several of his dogs took ill before he reached Dawson City and rather than push them he veered off the trail to visit friends. His unannounced arrival surprised his hosts and his initially unannounced scratch from the race surprised race officials.

For a long dog-team journey between the Yukon Territory and the Interior of Alaska in the dead of winter, the Quest offered surprisingly mild weather. The sky was mostly clear and the thermometer perched around minus 10 or 15 F (minus 23 to 27 C). Dogs love to run at those temperatures and performing tasks during stops is much easier for mushers.

Yet, the Quest still can humble competitors. From Mackey's and Dalton's sick dogs, to miscalculations made in carrying the proper amount of supplies as Buser and Cadzow did, mushers' plans are foiled. The unanticipated affects almost every musher's race at one time or another. Iris Wood Sutton of Tanana, Alaska, traveling at the back of the pack, was frustrated because her leaders rebelled . It took her nearly twenty-eight hours to cover the 201 miles from Pelly Crossing to Dawson City.

Jon Little remembered his first Quest in 2005. He studied the route and knew that there were several major hills, but until he reached Rosebud and Eagle Summits he didn't know what he would be asking of his dogs. "I had respect for them," Little said, "but I didn't know the team would have a meltdown on the steep hills at the end of a long race."

The 201-mile (323-km) gap between checkpoints is unique in mushing. "By the end of 150 miles you're going, 'God, I'd really like to see a checkpoint,'" Little said. "You just want somewhere to go, to have a cup of coffee, to talk to somebody."

Even though he was not racing, Turner drove to Dawson City, hung out, talked to mushers, and just enjoyed watching the dogs. During his many races, Turner had his share of hallucinations from sleep deprivation, but they were all vague, like seeing a light in the distance or a phantom dog team coming right at him.

For a while, Turner's biggest problem was brought on by his own idea of trying to find an edge. Not only did Turner drink a lot of coffee to help him stay awake on the trail, while he mushed he chewed on chocolate-covered coffee beans. He did not realize that caffeine was a diuretic that made him want to go pee quite often.

During one race, Turner and a half-dozen other mushers were trying to steal forty winks in a cabin. "Half of them were snoring in thirty seconds and half of them were freaking out because they couldn't fall asleep because the other guys were snoring," Turner said. "I would get up to pee and kick somebody in the head on the way by to stop the snoring. Accidentally, of course."

Remembering the rag-tag debut of Neff, now contending for the title, Turner appraised, "Hugh has come a long way."

The first rule of dog mushing, expressed in firm tones to every beginner musher, is to never let go of the sled. That means that even if dogs start to run away, hold on. That means even if dogs tip the sled and drag you through the snow, hold on.

Neff was kneeling by his team, pulling a bootie onto one dog's foot when the team spooked. Too late Neff grabbed for the sled handlebars. The dogs escaped and Neff chased, yelling the name of each dog as he plodded through the snow. It was like Santa Claus calling out the names of his reindeer.

"I almost lost my voice," Neff said. "I almost yelled every dog's name in the team. I was talking to God, that's for sure." Three miles down the trail, Neff caught up with his huskies only because the sled tipped over sideways and the dogs stopped.

Dogs on the loose are a nightmare. They can wreck a musher's race. Neff recovered and stayed in the hunt for the Quest championship.

This was more than could be said for Gatt. In a stunning development in Dawson City, the three-time champ, running in fourth place, announced he was dropping out of the race to concentrate on winning the Iditarod. No one could think of another example of a contending musher in the Quest or Iditarod quitting for no apparent reason other than lack of interest.

"It's never easy to scratch," Gatt said. "It goes against my belief to finish what you start." He said he had no regrets.

When the race leaders hit the trail again, Gatt hit the road in his dog truck.

CHAPTER FIFTEEN

RICK MACKEY'S QUEST

"The 1996 Yukon Quest was dedicated to Charlie Biederman, the last of the Alaskans who delivered the U.S. mail by dog sled in the 1930s and 1940s. Biederman had hoped to be at the start line of the race, but he died in late 1995, just after the Smithsonian had honored him in their new National Postal Museum in Washington, D.C." — John Firth, *Yukon Quest*

1996-1997 Rick Mackey grew up with sled dogs. His dad, Dick, helped Joe Redington organize the Iditarod Trail Sled Dog Race in 1973, competed in the first Iditarod, and won the closest Iditarod race ever — a one-second victory.

When Rick was a kid, the family lived in Anchorage, but the days when kennels were common within city limits are long gone in a city grown to 280,000 people, and Rick now lives in Nenana.

Dick Mackey worked days for the Alaska Railroad and when he came home from work Rick had the dogs prepared for a training run. The chore was part of Rick's after-school responsibilities. That immersed Rick in dog-sled culture from an early age. Long-distance races intrigued him, as they did his half-brothers, Lance and Jason. In 1983, Rick, almost literally following in his father's footsteps, became the second Mackey to win the Iditarod.

Despite being well established as a top-level musher, when Mackey went into town, to do some shopping in nearby Fairbanks, Quest fans used to tease him. "When are you going to run the hard race?" they asked.

As late as October of 1995, Mackey had not signed up for any 1996 long-distance races because he was low on sponsors. At the annual Fairbanks dog-mushing symposium he ran into Phil Cole, a friend who was executive director of the Quest's Alaska board that year. Cole was helping organize the following year's race and he challenged Mackey to make the run. Cole, also a local businessman, helped Mackey round up sponsors, so he entered his first Quest. Mackey hadn't had time for a thorough scientific study of the course, but decided to rely on his own experience and instincts.

In an interesting twist given future events, Quest officials announced before the 1996 race that any dog musher who could win their race and the Iditarod in the same mushing season would win a $50,000 bonus on top of other prize money. At the time, no one thought such an accomplishment was possible. Charlie Boulding, Bob Holder, and Sonny Lindner were the only mushers who had entered both events in the same year.

"It's not realistic," said Martin Buser, the Iditarod star, summarizing common thinking at the time.

Ramy Brooks, a Healy musher from a family with a long tradition of dog racing, signed up for both events, but later passed on the Quest while placing eleventh in the Iditarod.

Because he had the dog power, Mackey could stay close to front-runner John Schandelmeier, who had won one Quest title at the time. Thus, Mackey learned from an expert while on the run. It turned out that Mackey had latched onto the right guy. Schandelmeier captured the halfway award in Dawson, and nearly every other race trophy, including the Veterinarians' Choice Award and the Golden Harness Award. The Paxson musher won his second Quest, but by only fifty-eight minutes over Mackey.

Mackey spent the entire race quizzing Schandelmeier. "He taught me the trail, basically," Mackey said. "I stayed with him and questioned him. I'd say, 'Hey, what's next?' Or, 'Where are we going next?' That sort of thing. We had a good run. I probably would have felt bad if I beat him. He deserved to win, let's put it that way. He had a helluva team."

During the closing miles, Mackey had a near-mishap. Besides having difficulty trying to find some of the trail markers, he was confronted by a cow moose with a calf that jumped onto the trail in front of his team. Excited by the sight, the dogs picked up their pace in pursuit of the animals while Mackey tried to halt them. If the big moose turned back and went after the dogs, Mackey knew they would be in trouble. Fortunately, that did not happen and he went on to win $19,000 and the rookie-of-the-year award.

"I don't think I beat him on my race strategy," Schandelmeier said after pushing through to the Whitehorse finish line in one long 92-mile (148-km) run from Braeburn Lodge. "I had to beat him on dogs."

There were also many cheers for Kris Swanguarin, forty-two, a former Alaskan who had moved to Michigan, but then had to fight testicular cancer. As an affirmation of his return to strength, Swanguarin entered the 1996 Quest, finishing eleventh in just over fourteen days. "I guess what everyone wants to do is live a full life," he said. "Running the Quest will make my life fuller."

He was not the first — nor the last — to think that way.

Rick Mackey was intrigued enough by his success in 1996 to take another crack the following year. That was a much tighter race, with Schandelmeier, Frank Turner, and Mark May, whose father Joe won the 1980 Iditarod, in the lead pack with Mackey. Mackey stayed in the hunt even after oversleeping by more than four hours near the halfway point. "I thought I had totally blown it," he said. But Mackey recovered, having the experience of eighteen Iditarod races to draw upon. He had an additional obstacle to overcome that likely cost some time. Commander, one of his favorite leaders, was worn down and had to be carried for miles in the sled basket. "I had my work cut out for me when I left Dawson," Mackey said.

Mackey caught up at Slaven's Cabin. The others were surprised he made up so much time so quickly. The big move caught the leaders before they had all unrolled their bedding and that gave Mackey renewed confidence.

As sons of fathers who were early Iditarod racers, Mackey and May had known each other since their teenage years. Mackey started talking with May, asking how long they had been at the cabin, and how it was going. May replied, "We ain't been here long enough, and it's not going good enough. You got me, you son of a gun."

Heading towards Fairbanks, the quartet was bunched up approaching Eagle Summit. Turner led the last 20 miles (32 km) before the climb, but when he reached the base of the hill, he pulled his dogs off the trail and told Mackey he'd had enough, and urged Mackey to lead. Eagle Summit is notorious for its horrible weather and often is a make-or-break stretch in the Quest. Mackey did not want to lead. "I said, 'Frank, I don't even know if my dogs are going to go over this mountain, and you're not going to want to be right behind me if they spin around on us like some of the stories I've heard. You've got the veteran dogs. Go ahead over.' Nope, he wouldn't do it. He ended up sitting down behind his sled because the wind was blowing a little bit. He just crossed his arms and looked at me."

Turner told Mackey that it was his turn to break trail and neither of them budged. Schandelmeier and May caught up. After a brief pow-wow, the two decided to tackle the Summit together. A German film crew had taken a helicopter to the top seeking fancy footage and erected several tripods. May's team got tangled up and crashed into the tripods, knocking them over. Amid the chaos, Turner's team ended up in front, and just as he feared, his dogs rebelled against the icy hill, turned around, and began trotting down the hill the wrong way. To make matters worse, the dogs abandoned the trail and ran down an incline toward a ravine.

"He was in trouble, but he got them stopped and fixed it — it could have been horrible," Mackey said.

Schandelmeier surveyed the mess and told Mackey, "Well, Gin Gin will get us over." Gin Gin was his main leader. Years later Schandelmeier named a middle distance race after Gin Gin because of his admiration for the dog. Mackey followed Schandelmeier, but on a steep portion of the climb, his excited dogs started accelerating of their own volition and began running out of control. Mackey tried to slow them down, but they just ran faster.

"I actually passed him [Schandelmeier] going up Eagle Summit," Mackey said.

Mackey did not ask the team for more power, but the dogs gave it anyway. They were fast and strong and gave Mackey a lot of confidence. The four mushers were together again at the Mile 101 stop of the Steese Highway, and it was there that Mackey became convinced he would win.

Dick Mackey showed up to offer encouragement. He urged his son to pick up the pace on the run to the Angel Creek checkpoint, where an eight-hour rest was required. The younger Mackey recalled the conversation later. "He said, 'Why don't you get going? These guys are just getting rested.' And I said, 'Yeah, but I've got the fastest team, so it doesn't really matter. Once we pull out of here, I'm going to go faster than any of them.'"

The mile marker on the Steese Highway signified that ninety percent of the race was completed, and they were in the home stretch. "I was really hyped up," Mackey said of his dogs' speed and power. "I had a heck of a team. They were strong and they were about to kill me getting there. They were fast and they had a lot left."

Mackey had a twenty-five-minute lead at Angel Creek, aware that the last run to the Chena River finish line that year had been lengthened to 100 miles (161 km). Racing through populated areas where spectators have come out to the road to watch, sometimes mushers can obtain intelligence by asking how far they are behind the leader. But Mackey was the leader. Riding on the runners, he turned his head occasionally to glance over his shoulder. Only once did he spot two mushers in the far distance. He calculated they were an hour behind him.

May had to mush past his dog yard on the outskirts of town. His dogs thought they were going home, and May had to talk them out of it. The dogs got into a bit of a tangle. He wasn't going to catch Mackey anyway, but it dropped him a little bit farther back.

Mackey's winning time of 12 days, 5 hours, 55 minutes led Turner by one hour and eight minutes. Schandelmeier was five minutes behind Turner and May was 17 minutes behind him.

It is possible that papa Dick Mackey was happier about Rick's win than Rick was. "Any time your kids excel you just pop your buttons," Dick Mackey said.

THERE ARE ALWAYS sub-plots along the trail, individual experiences or events that stick with a musher who is not even in contention.

As a tribute to a late friend, Kathy Swenson, who did not finish the Quest that year, spread some of Tamara Lancaster's ashes along the trail. Suzan Amundsen, another friend of Lancaster's, distributed more ashes along the Iditarod trail.

That same year, the Quest was shaken by squabbling between the boards on each side of the international boundary. A race founded in the spirit of cooperation, linking history between Americans and Canadians, was close to destruction because of disputes involving money and politics. In the end, the citizen-officials followed the lead of the mushers who always help one another on the trail. When the wilderness threatens to overwhelm a musher and dogs, fellow mushers always step in to help. Sometimes that means giving a ride to a musher separated from his team, or stopping runaway dogs. Survival comes first. Likewise, survival of the race itself was paramount when new boards of directors came together.

Yet, for a short time, the Quest was in jeopardy. Alaska officials threatened to start an Alaska-only race to replace it while keeping the Quest name. Co-founder LeRoy Shank protested, saying the Quest was the Quest and others backing a new race should find their own name. Brian O'Donoghue, a Fairbanks journalist who had signed up to race in 1998, said he was going to mush the Fairbanks-to-Whitehorse route regardless.

"I won the last real one, I guess," Rick Mackey moaned.

Bob Eley, sports editor of the Fairbanks newspaper, recalls that when the entire Alaska board quit, remaining officials and volunteers were surprised to find $60,000 worth of unpaid bills in the office.

A call was made to true Quest believers. Eley served as president again for a one-year term. Funds were raised. The race was saved.

CHAPTER SIXTEEN

A GOLD RUSH CENTENNIAL

"The trees had been stripped by a recent wind of their white covering of the frost, and they seemed to lean toward each other, black and ominous, in the fading light. A vast silence reigned over the land." — Jack London, *White Fang*

1998 After the scare of the preceding summer, it was business as usual for the Quest in 1998. Rick Mackey was back to defend his title. Rick's daughter Brenda, just nineteen, joined him in the Quest starting field.

Rick was going after another victory. Brenda primarily wanted to finish and finish as high as she could. Even with the thirty-six-hour layover, father and daughter were running such different races they didn't overlap in Dawson. He was leaving from one end of town as she was pulling into the other. When he reached Eagle, the first Alaska checkpoint, they spoke by phone. That was their only contact on the trail. She said, "I know you're going to catch them, Dad." But Mackey said he was thinking, "Oh man, this ain't like last year." There were too many other good teams in the field.

The Quest had an added flavor in 1998, celebrating the 100th anniversary of the Klondike Gold Rush. That history had motivated Roger Williams to help organize the first Quest. Williams worked devotedly with the Quest. For five years he lived, slept, and breathed Quest, and then he decided he wanted to see what a normal life was like. He stepped back, moved to Mississippi where he grew up, and followed the race from afar.

"I just thank God for the Internet." Williams said.

Williams, who lost most of his Quest souvenirs in Hurricane Katrina in 2005, doesn't shrink from the description of the Yukon Quest as the toughest race around. It was supposed to be, he said. Many thought the Quest was going to be too tough for mushers to finish, until Sonny Lindner finished the first one. " 'Too hard,' they said," according to Williams. "'They're not going to be able to make it. You're going to kill a bunch of people.' When he [Lindner] crossed the finish line, that talk stopped. We wanted it to be a race that more reflected travel back there in gold-rush days."

The 1998 race celebrated that heritage. Mackey said he thought about the gold rush quite a bit that year. "On the Canadian side, there are quite a few old mines and there's old mining equipment left by the side of the trail," Mackey said. "You think, 'This is pretty neat. Them old-timers brought this stuff out here way back when and now I am passing by."

Mackey completed his third Quest in third place, behind Bruce Lee and Quebec musher Andre Nadeau. Brenda Mackey had her rookie struggles, but finished eighteenth, one of the youngest Quest finishers ever.

"It was a thrill," Mackey said of watching his daughter cross the finish line. "It's one of the highlights of our whole mushing career." That's saying something in the Mackey family.

No one came into the 1998 Quest with more determination than Bruce Lee, who had helped Jeff King get his racing start. Lee had been in the top five in the Quest several times. It still stung that Charlie Boulding had defeated him by five minutes in 1991. After running the Iditarod several times, the 1998 Quest was Lee's main focus. "That is the only race I have ever run in my life where the only thing that mattered to me was winning," Lee said. "The Quest is the only race I ever felt like I wanted to win so much. I did have a soft place in me for the Quest."

Lee and his wife, Jerylyn, spend summers working with the tourist industry near their Denali Park home. Winters, Lee mushed in the park's backcountry, seeing vistas few saw. His racing grew out of taking those long pleasure rides. From the time the snow began falling in early fall of 1997, Lee was serious about planning ahead. He even hired two handlers. "We've got only one goal this year and we're going to win this race," he told them.

The race included recent past champions John Schandelmeier, Frank Turner, and Rick Mackey. Lee figured that Mackey, the defending champion, would be his chief competition.

"We all knew he was tougher than nails," Lee said. "I called up and talked strategy with all of the mushers I respected who had a Quest background." More than anyone, he relied on advice from his friend Vern Halter, the 1990 champ. Mushing in the Fairbanks direction, Halter said Lee must shed Mackey by the time the race left the Yukon River.

"If he smells the finish line, and you're in sight, you know what Rick's like," Halter told Lee. "He will not stop." Lee sensed that Halter was correct. "There's something in those Mackey boys. They're tough to the core."

Lee admitted that he had screwed up by taking Charlie Boulding, then an unknown, too lightly in 1991. He was not going to make that kind of mistake again. With Mackey, Turner, and Schandelmeier running, it seemed clear this trio would be the ones to beat. Everyone thought so. And everyone was wrong. They overlooked a fresh face.

Almost nothing was known about newcomer Andre Nadeau from Quebec. He did not mingle much with the other mushers at the pre-race banquet or other events. His first language was French, and he gave the impression that his understanding of English was minimal. Later, it became apparent he spoke English better than he'd let on. Regardless of whether it was natural because of the circumstances, or whether Nadeau purposely cultivated the image, the French-Canadian came off as somewhat of a mystery man. He gave the impression that if he could make his dogs bark in French, he would have done so. The first time mushers and Quest officials saw Nadeau feed his dogs they were baffled. He threw whole, frozen chickens, feathers and all, to his dogs at dinnertime.

"Everything he did was so unconventional that people made jokes about him," Lee said.

Lee didn't laugh, however, when Nadeau started the race at a blistering pace and ran his team for ten to twelve hours at a time without much rest. Like everyone else, Lee believed that if Nadeau tried to keep up that pace for long, he would drop out. Lee felt certain Nadeau would implode.

"Someone can do that repeatedly for a Kuskokwim 300 race, or in a 400-mile race," Lee said, "but they aren't going to do it for 1,000 miles. I took my knowledge of dogs and compared it and decided I was going to stick with my own schedule. I was not going to start chasing because I could see that I was traveling faster when my dogs got more rest. But I took him totally seriously." The Boulding lesson reverberated.

Experience in the longest races sometimes puts mushers into a rut. Something has worked before, so they don't want to tamper with success, but periodically, as the Iditarod and Quest progressed, mushers dared to be different. They broke open the race unexpectedly by going longer without rests, or by altering their run-rest schedules. More than one musher has lost a championship by being too cautious. It's part of the challenge to know when to change strategy and make bold moves and when to hold back and husband resources for the late going. A musher confronted with a maverick strategy must use all his will power not to be thrown off. It was tempting for Lee to run faster, earlier, in pursuit of Nadeau. But he had to demonstrate belief in his own plan and know that his dogs would be stronger when it counted farther down the trail, based on the way they had trained. Still, there was a what-if voice lurking at the edge of his mind. Falling behind by too far early in the race could be fatal.

Lee trusted his own background and his own math rather than being swayed by Nadeau's pace. "I looked at the speed I was running," Lee said. "I checked the times. I would see that he left this point and got to that point and then I got there. I could figure out that I was running forty-five minutes to an hour faster every run and was getting more rest. I was just going to keep doing what I was doing until I felt it was time to drop the hammer, and then I could skip a rest break."

What no one besides his wife knew was that in the early part of the race, Lee had dropped two of his main leaders. One pulled a muscle stepping in a crack on the ice and the other just started limping. It was like suiting up a basketball team without the two best players. None of Lee's other dogs had the leadership experience needed for the Quest trail.

Jerylyn gave Lee a pep talk: maybe a couple of the other dogs will emerge as top-flight leaders. Lee didn't believe that for a minute, so when he mushed into Pelly Crossing in second place, he was surprised. "How can that be?" he thought. "I can't be the second one here because things didn't go that well."

The only other musher into Pelly Crossing ahead of Lee was Nadeau. Lee wondered where Mackey and the others were, but only for a minute. He was in second place and it was time to make a move. Lee finally passed Nadeau near Biederman's Cabin, home of the pioneer sled-dog mailman Charlie Biederman, about 80 miles (129 km) shy of Circle. Lee would not be passed again.

The true measure of a good dog team is taken in the hills and mountains that make mushers climb more than 3,000 feet (915 meters), not when the weather is calm and the trail smooth. Lee feared that he would miss his experienced leaders when the mushing got tough. This thought hovered in the back of his mind, and then he reached Eagle Summit. It was fresh in Lee's mind that Gerald Riley, the veteran musher, had confronted that big hill in a previous Quest and watched his dogs quit on him. Riley ended up bringing them home in the dog truck.

Eagle Summit is steep and the wind blows viciously. Storms arise seemingly without warning. Lee's young leaders eyed the terrain and stopped. "They just didn't want to go," he said. " I switched the dogs around. They took ten steps and they'd stop. I had had dogs for twenty years that had run in every kind of weather condition. I had to find the answer in my background to get those dogs over the Summit. We were either going to scratch there or we were going to get over. There was no middle ground. "

Lee moved his balky leaders farther back in the team, clipping them into the middle of the harness. He moved two other dogs into lead position. The sled moved in fits. He removed some of his gear from the sled to ease the load. The dogs moved a little. Finally, Lee unloaded almost all of his equipment, nearly emptying the sled. In the process, he began sweating heavily in his warm outer clothing. So he removed his parka.

Rather than a smoothly operating dog-sled team, Lee's actions approximated a climber on Mount McKinley taking three steps forward at one time and stopping to breathe while ferrying loads between camps. "I tried pushing the sled," Lee said. "I tied a long rope onto the snow hook and went up by the leaders. I pulled and let them just walk. "

It was cold, but Lee was generating sweat by the gallon. He took off his outer layer of clothing, folded everything, and placed it ahead on the hill. He carried his cooker up the hill. He made a cache 100 yards (91 meters) from the lead dog and pushed the sled ten steps at a time. Inch by inch, he conquered the hill. The dogs trotted as far as the stacked-up gear, then stopped.

"We got into the baby-step thing," Lee said. "As long as they could see a target, they went to it."

So Lee repeated the process. Tote the gear up the hill, make a nice, neat little pile, then drive the dogs to the gear. Hours passed. While he worked with the dogs and carried loads, Lee glanced behind him, waiting for Nadeau to appear any second. "It felt like an eternity," Lee said. "I kept looking for him. I saw this whole year's work, this whole race, falling through my fingers at that point."

Lee worked to exhaustion. His muscles ached. He was stressed from the activity. When the dogs began moving short distances, though, Lee got excited. This plan, Plan D, or whatever it was, was working. It was a rewarding thing to see, and after a while he was positive his team was going to make it over Eagle Summit.

"Your lungs are burning, your legs are tired, I was soaking wet," Lee said. "The musher is the weak point in the team."

At last, at last, the dogs, the sled, and the musher were atop Eagle Summit, 3,685 feet (1,124 meters) above sea level. As soon as they reached the top, a blast of wind ripped right through Lee, reminding him that he was standing in sub-zero cold and that he no was longer wearing his warmest clothing, most of which was down the hill, where he had left it in a neat pile. With a wind like this, the cold would freeze him within minutes. If he left the dogs alone, they might run off, or run back down the hill. But he needed to do something quickly, so he gave the dogs snacks, dug in his snow hook, and ran down the hill. He scooped up his equipment, including the cooker, and climbed to the top once more. "That was really risky, but I couldn't go on without things," he said.

If the dogs had followed him back down the hill, Lee knew he never would have been able to get them to climb a second time. The best news for him during this ordeal, though, was that Nadeau never materialized. That was more of a transitory thought because, by then, Lee's big-picture concern was frostbite. He had no feeling at all in his nose and when he touched its tip, it felt like a rock. His hands started to go numb, and the wind preyed upon his sweat. In an earlier race, Lee had been with Jeff King on American Summit when King frostbit his left hand. Lee remembered King parking his team and saying, "I'm in big trouble." When King showed Lee his hand, "it looked like something pulled out of a freezer." The memory motivated Lee to bundle up quickly.

"I realized this was one of those points when I had about two minutes to deal with the situation or I wasn't going to be able to take care of myself," Lee said. "I knew this could end for me right there. The dogs were very well behaved. They were just resting, eating their snacks — bars made of a frozen mixture of ground beef, fats, and oil with commercial dog food and some liver in it. I just jumped into my gear."

Lee was as protected from the howling wind as he could be. When he was dressed, he yelled to the dogs, "Let's go!" and mushed as fast as he could away from Eagle Summit. He was not safe yet, however. His hands bothered him and he still sweated under the parka. For the next hour, he feared for his health, wondering if his hands would be frostbitten and if he might become hypothermic. Then, he hit the Mile 101 checkpoint on the Steese Highway and his mood instantly lifted.

"I was very, very relieved," Lee said.

Calming down, organizing his thoughts, and replaying what just had happened, Lee realized he had come through a very dangerous place. It was possible that Nadeau, who had disappeared from view, was at risk on the summit. "The first thing I said to the officials was, 'If Andre isn't here in about an hour, you ought to go look for him because it's not good up there right now,'" Lee said. "I thought about being a rookie up there and, man, it wasn't just that the dogs had a hard time."

At Mile 101, officials had a barrel stove going with a raging fire. Lee stripped down again and dried himself and his gear. "I was spent and went in and lay down," he said.

He needed the nap, but Lee did not forget he was racing. As soon as he was recharged, he was back on the trail, leading the way into Fairbanks. He didn't let up and he did not underestimate Nadeau. However, when Lee was zipping along the frozen Chena River near downtown Fairbanks, he stopped looking behind him and realized he was going to win. Alone in the frigid night he took a few minutes to savor his accomplishment. Gliding over the frozen surface on his sled runners, he snapped off his headlamp and went invisible, except for the reflection of his team in the moonlight. It was a sweet moment.

"It did feel good," Lee said. "The thing I'm happiest about is that I recognized the moment. A lot of people, no matter their goal in life, live without conscious recognition. They might not realize 'til later that something special has occurred. It was just a very quiet, personal moment. I remember thinking; 'I will never be in this point in time with these dogs again.' And then we came around a bend in the river and there was Fairbanks all lit up."

Lee was forty-four when he won the Quest and the $30,000 prize. But in the 2000s he stepped back from mushing, sold off the dogs in his kennel, and worked as either a race judge or a TV consultant on the Iditarod during the race season while shifting his winter base to New Mexico.

Former Quest champion Joe Runyan, Lee, and several other retired Iditarod and Quest mushers established an expatriate colony of sorts near the Gila National Forest on the outskirts of Silver City, an historic mining town. Instead of driving dog teams, the men have get-togethers riding mules or horses through the dry and warm backcountry.

"When you're sitting on a horse up on a mesa looking out across the New Mexico landscape and talking about dog mushing — we do it all the time — it cracks us up," Lee said.

Neither Lee nor the others miss snow and ice much, but he does miss the rugged northern country and history. "Seeing the mountains and the big lakes and rivers and no one's out there, that was my favorite part of the Quest," he said.

He strongly believes the official international border separating the Yukon Territory and Alaska is manufactured. The homesteaders who live on each side of the line in Pelly Crossing or Eagle are the same kind of people who represent the closest ties between the United States and Canadian entities, and they are Yukon Quest mushers.

"Mushers, officials, people from the newspapers that cover the race, the people that are involved with that event, that is where the spirit of the old Yukon is kept alive," Lee said. "It isn't Alaska. It isn't the Yukon. It's the North. It's the northern culture."

CHAPTER SEVENTEEN

ALASKA NATIVE HERO

"They quickened the old life within him, the old tricks which they had stamped into the heredity of the breed were his tricks..." – Jack London, *Call of the Wild*

1999   Ramy Brooks was brought up in Interior Alaska with a yard full of puppies that might as well have been his brothers and sisters. If any musher in the Yukon Quest and Iditarod was destined to race dogs, it was Brooks.

His mother is Roxy Wright, one of the greatest sprint-mushing champions in Alaska history. His grandfather is Gareth Wright, who won his last North American Open Sled Dog Championship in Fairbanks thirty-three years after winning his first one. The elder Wright pioneered the breed of Aurora huskies that so many mushers race.

Mushing was in Brooks's blood and training was in his upbringing. But after high school as he moved into his twenties, he decided he had to explore the larger world. He left Alaska for a spell, joined the Navy, but was lured back to the North by the land and, yes, the dogs.

In the 1990s, the demographics of long-distance mushing were changing, particularly in the Iditarod. With more attention on the event and with the best mushers acquiring corporate sponsors, Alaska Natives like Brooks were being squeezed out of the race. Those who lived off the road system and who had to fly their dogs and supplies everywhere for races had trouble keeping up with the costs. One by one, most of the top Eskimo and Athabascan mushers pulled back from the Iditarod. Village economies offered few opportunities for high-paying jobs needed to pay for new, improved equipment, transportation, and enriched dog food. It was hard to keep up with the Joneses when the Joneses had kennels of 100 dogs to choose from. Nobody in the Bush could afford the high price of maintaining such a kennel.

Yet Brooks stood out when he appeared on the scene. He was one of few Natives who had the backing to make a dent in the Iditarod standings. He made his debut in the Iditarod in 1994, finishing seventeenth, and was named rookie of the year. From that moment on, he became a sort of Great Native Hope, a statewide symbol of a Native musher who could compete. He was a fresh face and Brooks's squeaky-clean image was of a family man with his wife, Cathy, and three young children. He did not drink or smoke, leading Alaska Native leaders to single him out for anti-substance abuse and stay-in-school campaigns.

Soft-spoken and thoughtful, Brooks might well have preferred staying out of the limelight, but accepted his role of responsibility and made numerous appearances for these worthy causes. A higher profile afforded him much needed sponsorship as well.

Brooks placed sixteenth in the Iditarod in 1995, eleventh in 1996, eighth in 1997, and eighteenth in 1998. He was learning his trade, placing well, and winning prize money, but seemingly treading water. In 1999, Brooks decided to take a break from the Iditarod and transfer his focus to the Yukon Quest. His life was in transition that year. While he was selling off his house in Fairbanks, he temporarily relocated to Eureka, Alaska, home of Susan Butcher and Dave Monson, and shared a training base there.

"My kennel was a lot smaller," Brooks said. "I had sixteen race-age dogs and I felt I didn't have the depth to go to the Iditarod. I felt I had a solid core and allowing for the possibility of three or four of them getting injured or not working out. I could count on twelve. That wasn't a whole lot of wiggle room. I had been looking at the Quest and thought I could go there. I went with the idea that I was going there to win."

There was a field of twenty-nine entered chasing the $30,000 first prize and a huge crowd of several thousand sent the mushers off to the Yukon from the Chena River in 1999. Chief contenders were past champions Frank Turner, John Schandelmeier, and Mark May, forty-nine, a veterinarian living in North Pole, Alaska, near Fairbanks.

ONE OF THE OTHER entries was Sepp Herrmann, a transplanted German musher who, the previous November had survived the horror of a grizzly-bear attack on his dog team in Alaska's Brooks Range.

Herrmann was lucky to survive. At one point, as the bear was eating one of his dogs, Herrmann reached for his only suitable weapon — a snow hook on the sled — but the furious bear came after him. Herrmann said the bear stood on its hind legs, placed its paws on his shoulders, and seemed about to tear him apart. Herrmann shouted into the bear's face, and one of his dogs bit the bear on the butt. The bear turned and killed the dog, but Herrmann escaped.

Making his way to the Dalton Highway, Herrmann hitchhiked into the tiny community of Wiseman. Herrmann rounded up a posse of armed local residents and returned to the scene. The bear was still there, devouring the dogs one at a time. One of the men accompanying Herrmann shot and killed the bear. It was too late for all but one dog — the severely injured Zulu.

Herrmann had been running trap-line dogs that helped him make his living, so when the bear killed eight dogs, tragic as it was, the episode not only appeared likely to ruin his race hopes, but also to severely affect his livelihood. When word of the bear attack spread, there was an outpouring of help. Cash donations from Germany and other aid from all over the world made it possible for Herrmann to rebuild his team sufficiently enough to complete a Quest qualifying event in fifth place and to enter the big race. A sled-maker presented him with a new sled. The support brought Herrmann to the starting line but he was haunted by the attack

"The whole thing is sticking in my bones," he said.

Using his makeshift team, Herrmann placed fifteenth, won $1,500, and earned the Veterinarians Choice Award, emblematic of the vets' feeling that he took the best care of his dogs along the trail.

Herrmann's personal odyssey to complete the Quest in 1999 is evidence that everybody in the race is somebody. Each musher — not just winners — carries into the wild the hopes and dreams of armchair adventurers everywhere. The mushers on the finishers' list represent those who cross the line from dreamer to doer. By definition, they are risk-takers, and often their stories are as compelling as the winner's.

Meanwhile, Brooks, then thirty, was in the Quest to test himself, to prove to himself that he could win the major title that had eluded him in the Iditarod. Brooks had one Quest under his belt, but felt that he was six years smarter than he was in his 1993 debut. The temperatures were not as extreme as usual on the trail in 1999. Brooks got the drop on the other mushers and set the early pace. When he cruised the 150 miles (241 km) from Eagle to the halfway mark in Dawson City, he had built more than a three-hour lead on May.

Leaving Dawson, Brooks said he made a couple of mistakes on the unfamiliar Quest trail. He misjudged how far it was to a good resting spot and paused too soon, forcing him and his dogs to make a longer run to even out his schedule. May had broken up his run a little better and gained on Brooks.

By the time he got to Carmacks, Brooks sensed May was making his move. "I was starting to question whether or not I had what was needed to win." Brooks said. "He was getting ready to leave before I did. I wanted to rest a full eight hours, and still I had a half-hour to rest. I sat there for a few minutes and thought, 'We're getting too close to the finish line. I can't let him just go out of here and give him the lead.' So I went out."

Following the trail across a series of lakes, Brooks looked over his shoulder and saw May in the distance stalking him. "He was getting bigger and bigger, like he was gaining on me," Brooks said. "I'm thinking, 'Maybe the team is done for,' but if you start thinking defeat, it will transfer to the dogs so easily. I watched him for an hour or so as he slowly gained on me, but then I thought, 'This is one heck of a dog team in front of me. I'm not just gonna give up.'"

He stopped his dogs, snacked them on salmon, and Brooks shifted them around in harness, ending up with Pretty Boy and Dylan in dual lead. May had closed to about 300 yards (274 meters) by the time the dogs finished their snack break. Brooks gave a whistle, the dogs jumped to their feet, and for the first time in the race he asked them to run hard.

Brooks came into the Braeburn Lodge checkpoint, no longer seeing May, but with trouble seeing the marked trail. If he got lost then, he was going to lose the race. Brooks stepped inside to eat and soon May showed up. Mom Roxy Wright was handling for Brooks and as she went to the counter to get him a dessert, she walked past May's table. He looked up and said, "What's that boy of yours got? He must have a turbocharger on that team."

Brooks knew then he would be okay. Entering the required eight-hour Braeburn layover, he had a thirty-four-minute lead on May with about 100 miles (161 km) of racing left. At Takhini Hot Springs, the trail led back onto the Yukon River. Brooks tried to spot May, but had no idea how close he was trailing due to the frequent turns on the frozen river.

"When I whistled those dogs up, I showed I believed in them and they took off for me," Brooks said. "That had to be kind of demoralizing for him [May] and very positive for me. The momentum had been shifting for him. That was where the race was going to be won or lost."

Not so many hours later, Brooks mushed his dog team across the finish line in Whitehorse. He was right to worry about May because May had closed to within ten minutes of Brooks' winning time of 11 days, 8 hours, 27 minutes.

"I'm pretty proud," said Roxy Wright, who was on hand to witness her son claim the championship.

Brooks said winning the race was an emotional high that has stayed with him over the years. "It was a pretty incredible feeling to know that you had just won one of the major distance races in the world," he said. "It was very gratifying. I went into the race believing I had a good dog team. I believed I could win the Quest, or at least be a top three team."

At thirty, Brooks was the youngest Quest winner and the first Alaska Native champion. The victory was a confidence-builder for him.

Brooks turned his attention back to the Iditarod in the ensuing years, placing as high as second, before an ugly, inexplicable incident near the end of the 2007 race resulted in him being banned from the event. In the village checkpoint of Golovin, Brooks kicked a dog. Whether the reason was frustration or anger, there was no excuse. Likely, Brooks, who had previous difficulties with sleep deprivation on the trail, was worn to a frazzle. It was a shocking occurrence, so at odds with the image of the genial Brooks. He appeared to have simply snapped from stress.

The Iditarod levied a two-year suspension, a ban honored by other major races, including the Quest. The ban has expired, but Brooks, forty-one, has not expressed a desire to race again any time soon. He is developing a bed-and-breakfast business in Healy, managing a kennel of fifty dogs that allows him to lease teams to prospective Iditarod mushers, and offer sled-dog rides to tourists. At the same time, he commutes more than 100 miles (161 km) each way to Fairbanks to work part-time on a college degree at the University of Alaska Fairbanks. Brooks said he wants to set up an energy consulting business.

His priorities are family, school, and career. He has no idea whether he will race in the Quest or the Iditarod again, if he will subject his body to the rigors of the trail, and get his mind into competitive mode again. But Brooks knows he will stay in the sport some way.

"I love dog mushing," Brooks said. "I'll run dogs whether I'm racing or not is how I look at it."

CHAPTER EIGHTEEN

A WOMAN'S TURN

"I couldn't believe it was happening. It took weeks to hit me that I'd won the Iditarod."
— Libby Riddles, first woman to win the Iditarod.

2000 It happens with some frequency. Aliy Zirkle will be shopping at a store in Fairbanks, or giving a talk somewhere about dog mushing, and a little girl about eight or nine will say hello, and reveal that her name is Aliy, too. This is no coincidence. After Zirkle became the first woman to win the Yukon Quest in 2000, mothers inspired by the achievement named their just-born daughters after the champ.

Zirkle is taken aback by that form of celebrity status, but says that in the big-picture level of American society celebrityhood, "I always say I'm as famous as Kobe Bryant's big toe." Given the amount of exposure the Los Angeles Lakers basketball star receives, she may be right. Zirkle is probably a better basketball player than Bryant is a musher, anyway.

Zirkle, one of the many Alaskan mushers based in Two Rivers, previewed her capabilities in the 1999 race when she placed fourth — a move up from her previous seventeenth place standing the year before. So, leading up to the 2000 race, it was not crazy to think Zirkle might make the jump to first.

Women always have been involved in the Quest, especially on the administrative side, where several hold key positions, but no woman had come close to winning the championship. Lorrina Mitchell, a Quest organizer in Canada, was the first woman to finish the race when she placed eleventh in the inaugural event in 1984.

In 1985, the Iditarod gained international attention when Libby Riddles became the first woman to capture the crown in that 1,100-mile (1,770-km) run across Alaska. The biggest surprise was that the first woman was not Alaskan Susan Butcher, who already had been runner-up, and who won four of the next five races. Yet, although Willow musher DeeDee Jonrowe has placed second twice and has a number of top-five finishes, there hasn't been a female Iditarod champion since Butcher's last win in 1990. A decade later, no woman had come close to winning the Quest.

"We were starting to think, 'Is it ever going to happen?'" said Yukon musher Michelle Phillips, who had placed as high as fourth. Phillips was quite pleased when Zirkle won and she has experienced some of the same phenomenon of having little girls identify her as a role model. "I really think that they look up to you," Phillips said. "They say, 'You're my hero.' It really feels good. I say to the kids, 'You can do it.'"

A native of New Hampshire who also lived in Puerto Rico, Zirkle became a biologist after attending the University of Pennsylvania. Her first experience in Alaska was as a U. S. Fish and Wildlife volunteer in the remote community of Bettles on the south side of the Brooks Range. It did not take her long to acquire her first dog, a husky named Skunk, who became the inspiration for the name of her kennel — Skunk's Place.

Zirkle, who has a 1,000-watt smile, an exuberant manner, and long blonde hair, all of which draw attention to her, got her start in village races. After some middle-distance events, she made her Quest debut in that 1998 race at age twenty-eight.

While some might have given Zirkle consideration as a potential contender in 2000, most race observers felt the winner would be Frank Turner, Thomas Tetz, or Peter Butteri. Zirkle did nothing in the early going to suggest otherwise when she went out slowly. Tetz, one of the transplanted Germans, was living in Tagish. He was the underdog. A rugged athlete who had competed in the Ironman Triathlon, his kennel was low-budget. He spent just $2,000 acquiring his team. He protested that there was no way he would be competitive. But he was.

"I go out conservative and come on strong," said Zirkle. "I never travel with anyone. The Quest taught me that. I traveled with John Schandelmeier and Frank Turner, champions of the '90s and some of the good old boys. They're pretty hard-core, serious fellows. They are more competitive than they let on, so if you camp with them, they toy with you mentally. You learn pretty quickly not to camp with them anymore."

Head games are what Zirkle experienced. One of the guys would say, "Man, that dog looks sore. Is he sore? I wouldn't go with that dog. Hey, you might need to carry it." They made off-hand remarks that could put doubt in the mind of a less-experienced musher. Once, Turner came up to Zirkle at her camp and said, "What are you camping here for? If I were you I'd go up a quarter of a mile. There's a spruce tree on the left and a birch on the right. That's where I always camp."

Turner might have been merely acting friendly, offering sage advice to a younger musher, but Zirkle said she wanted to do things her way. "I'm like, 'Crap, I'm just going by hours, Frank. I don't know the trail like you do.' I had my own schedule."

Headed toward Whitehorse, Zirkle ignored any male posturing, sticking to her own strategy. At the halfway point, Zirkle took stock and began to believe her dogs were good enough to lead her to the championship. "That team was made up of very tough dogs," she said. "A lot of the dogs I had raced in Bush Alaska. I didn't have a big kennel, so I knew twelve of them intimately. They were very tough. They were not fast. Everyone had a faster team than I did, Peter Butteri and Thomas, for sure, and Frank probably did. But anything I asked my dogs to do, they did."

On the Stewart River, during the 200-mile (321-km) run between Dawson and Pelly Crossing, Canadian park rangers set up an old Army tent and put some spruce boughs down on the ground in case a musher wanted a nap. It provided an illusion of warmth at minus-50 F (-46 C) degrees. Zirkle felt she had to keep moving. "I hated Stewart River because it was always 50 below," she said. "The Canadian Rangers, bless their hearts, would say, 'Hey, if you want to use it, just light the stove.' They said it as if they had provided you with something. The mushers are supposed to be like, 'Yeah!' No way are you going to be warm. So I decided there was no reason to stop there except if you wanted to drop a dog. I had a plan to make the run in three stretches, not four, and that pretty much left everyone else resting more than me."

That turned out to be the game-winning move. "When I got through (Stewart River), I was way ahead of everyone," Zirkle said. "I knew if I didn't screw up, my team was probably tougher and stronger, and I could skimp on the rest more than they could."

Zirkle's winning time was 10 days, 22 hours, 57 minutes, just a half-hour ahead of Tetz. Turner finished third, another four hours back, and Butteri was fourth. That trio chased Zirkle all of the way into Takhini Hot Springs, which was designated the finish line that year on the outskirts of Whitehorse because of excessive open water approaching the capital city. But no one could catch her. Zirkle ran the last eighty miles straight through. "I had a plan going into the whole thing," she said. "We stuck to that plan."

Zirkle was able to conquer the main enemy of moving fast on the trail – sleep deprivation. Like anyone else trying to make do on too little rest, she has suffered from the problem. "It always plays a role," Zirkle said, "in making your decisions. I fed the dogs three meals instead of two, so they were running slower. I have put leaders on the wrong side of the team, a dog that is better as a right-hand leader and now she might drag me off the side of a cliff."

One of Zirkle's best weapons against fatigue, to prevent her from over-staying in checkpoints, was to wear two watches. When she beds down for a nap, she removes one, sets an alarm, and places it inside her beaver hat, right next to her ear. When the buzzing starts and won't stop, she knows it's time to get up, put booties on the dogs, and hit the trail.

Weary, but happy, Zirkle quickly realized she was not going to blend in with previous Yukon Quest winners. A girl had beaten the boys at their own game for the first time in the Quest and for the first time in a long time in long-distance mushing. When Libby Riddles won the Iditarod, it created an international hullabaloo, and Riddles received considerable attention from *Sports Illustrated* and other media. When Zirkle won the Quest, she saw signs of excitement right there in the Yukon.

"Coming across the finish line, there were hordes of women cheering me on and being very emotional," Zirkle said. "It opened my eyes right away. There were many people out there bearing small tokens, things showing it meant so much to them."

First place brought Zirkle $30,000. The act of winning was priceless. She has reflected over the years about how special it was to be the first woman to win the Quest, and what it's meant to others.

"You know, I live in a really small world," she said. "I live in Interior Alaska. I float around between Denali National Park and into Canada and Interior villages. That is, geographically, a big area with a small population. When I go to Fort Yukon, or Beaver and Say 'Hi, I'm Aliy,' people say, 'I know who you are.' I'm not hosting 'Saturday Night Live,' and I didn't merchandise myself much with the Quest win, but people know me."

Riddles telephoned congratulations when Zirkle became a champ. When Riddles won her championship, T-shirts mocking rough, tough Bushmen were printed and sold. They read, "Alaska, Where Men Are Men and Women Win the Iditarod." Zirkle joked that if anyone wanted to make a new version, subbing Yukon Quest for Iditarod, she will help print them.

Still, Zirkle switched to the Iditarod in 2001. She never defended her Quest crown, and no other woman has come close to winning. Zirkle believes that top-five placer Michelle Phillips might be the next female champion. "Michelle Phillips is really knocking on the door right now," Zirkle said. "She's very dog-conscious, dog-friendly, kind of a happy gal. She certainly could pull something off."

When she is not mushing, Zirkle makes motivational speeches, sometimes in warm-weather climates where the audience members flinch as she describes doing outdoor chores in the severe Alaska-Yukon weather. Each summer during the tourist season, she comes home to Two Rivers for a special gig in nearby Fairbanks — greeting Alaska Railroad trains and giving talks to visitors, mostly about mushing.

Zirkle speaks to about 10,000 visitors a year. The demand for her autograph is so great that she pre-signs postcards before meeting the train to avoid being overwhelmed. "I was told I could get a hand stamp with my name, but I think that's cheating," Zirkle said. "My name is pretty easy. It's just Aliy."

Just Aliy. And everyone in the North knows who that is.

CHAPTER NINETEEN

DOING A DOUBLE

"Sitka Charley had achieved the impossible." — Jack London, *The Wisdom of the Trail*

2001   Tim Osmar was a mushing prodigy. As a teenager he won three Junior Iditarod titles. His father, Dean, won the Iditarod in 1984, and then retired. When the younger Osmar began to race the long event at eighteen as a rookie in 1985, it was suggested that he was going to be the youngest musher ever to capture the crown in the race from Anchorage to Nome.

It didn't work out that way, but after years of placing in the top five, top ten, top twenty, Osmar wrote history of a different sort in the 2001 Quest. What was once thought to be an impossible task had been proven possible by other mushers. Yes, a musher could complete the Yukon Quest and the Iditarod in the same year.

Yet, the feat was seen as an oddity because the few mushers who did so finished out of the prize money in at least one of the races, if not both. Osmar had a different goal in mind when he entered the Quest in 2001. He thought his dogs were championship material, and that between his kennel and his father's dogs, he had enough top-tier dogs to make a respectable run at both crowns in the same winter.

Osmar was a youngster of about twelve when he first mushed a dog team. Working the family's commercial fishing business in the waters off of Alaska's Kenai Peninsula he lived an outdoor life. In those days, the Osmars lived in Clam Gulch, a flyspeck of a community about 150 miles (241 km) from Anchorage. Fishing was a summer livelihood. Mushing dogs was a complementary activity.

It was natural that young Tim would follow his father in both endeavors.

After the elder Osmar won the Iditarod, he retired from long-distance competition, though he kept raising dogs. It was almost like flicking a light switch. I won, I'm done. That fast. There was considerable curiosity about what a young pup like Tim could do when he made his Iditarod debut. Finishing thirteenth garnered some attention. After all, he was just a kid. Boy, wait until this fella gains trail experience, older mushers said.

Young Osmar was heavyset and strong, much wider than his slender father. He had power in the shoulders, developed from hauling nets. And he had good instincts with the dogs. Osmar skipped the 1986 Iditarod and entered his first Quest. He finished third, won $5,000, added to his mushing education, and gained confidence. In 1987, Osmar had a breakthrough, finishing fourth in the Iditarod, a tremendous achievement for a twenty-year-old in his second race. The prophecy that he would be the next great Iditarod musher seemed within his reach.

However, hard lessons on the trail followed. There is no such thing as anointing a champion. Conditions dictate success. Experience always matters. Osmar placed third in 1992 and four times finished fourth in the Iditarod. Throughout the 1990s, he always finished in the top twenty, earning a payday, but felt he was in a rut because he had recorded no single great performance.

Meanwhile, Tim was no longer a boy wonder. He was married now, he and his wife, Tawny, had four children who were growing up fast, and the family moved to its own home in nearby Ninilchik. Osmar was not about to forsake the Iditarod, but he remembered how good it felt to do well in the 1986 Quest, and he decided to give it another crack. So, in 2001, he signed up to run both races.

While everyone knew that Osmar planned to run in both events, no one knew what resources he would devote to the Quest. Respected by reputation, his dogs were an unknown factor. Would he race his finest athletes in the Quest or save them for the Iditarod?

Approaching Dawson City, Osmar made it clear that his team had to be reckoned with. Over the final miles, he slipped past William Kleedehn and mushed into the checkpoint two minutes ahead to claim the four ounces of gold. Osmar had made his point: he was not back in the Quest for nostalgic reasons. Still, Osmar was well versed in the disappointments suffered in long races by leaders who took things for granted. He felt his chances to win were good, but he did not permit confidence to overtake prudence on the trail between Dawson and Fairbanks.

Osmar kept up a steady pace during the second half of the race, watching over his shoulder for a challenger. Indeed, someone did appear. Kleedehn fell back to third as Andrew Lesh of Fairbanks made a charge. Osmar's winning time of 11 days, 14 hours, 38 minutes was a mere 1 hour and 26 minutes ahead of Lesh. It might have been closer still, but Lesh was slapped with a thirty-minute penalty when he reached Angel Creek because of a rules violation committed in Carmacks. Lesh had gone to his truck to get sled repair tools. That is a no-no. The Quest rules state that a musher may only employ what he has with him in his sled or has shipped ahead on the trail to checkpoints via supply planes.

Osmar was gleeful at the finish line on the Chena River. "Everything was perfect," said Omar, who notched his first major title at age thirty-three. "Nothing could go wrong."

Nothing did go wrong. Osmar had kept his mind remarkably clear during the final run. He did not allow himself to celebrate victory in his head until he had victory secured in his thickly mittened hands. "I didn't even want to think about it," he said, "and the last ten miles were pretty long."

Osmar, as many finishers do, arrived in downtown Fairbanks under a night sky shortly before 4 a.m. He earned a deep sleep, but not long-term relaxation. Conveniently, the Quest ended in Alaska that year, so all Osmar had to do was load up his dogs and family and drive the 360 miles (579 km) to Anchorage to prepare for the 2001 Iditarod. That race was a week away — Osmar's next quest.

Osmar's training ground is the Caribou Hills, the vast wilderness that is essentially his backyard on the Kenai Peninsula. Mushing up the hills was good for building stamina in the dogs, though those bumps couldn't compare with climbs the stature of American Summit, Eagle Summit, Rosebud Summit, and King Solomon's Dome on the Quest Trail. Still, Osmar believed that type of terrain aided preparation.

"The hills helped me get a bit of an edge," Osmar said. "I figured all along I had just as good a chance as anybody."

That might not have been true doing the Iditarod back to back. Osmar had pulled off one leg of the difficult double title by winning the Quest. But he was going against well-rested mushers and their fresh dogs in the Iditarod. The feeling remained unchanged in public opinion: no one performs really well in both the Quest and the Iditarod in the same year.

Initially, it had been not part of Osmar's seasonal strategy to enter both races. The Caribou Hills practice runs had showed Osmar his dogs were quite powerful, but they did not seem to have the speed he would have ideally liked for the faster paced Iditarod. He was torn between matching the dogs' running styles with the Quest and skipping the Iditarod altogether for a year. It was his dad Dean, who blurted out, "You should do both."

Osmar brought a relaxed attitude to the Iditarod starting line. "We already had a good year," he said. "It wasn't the Iditarod, but it was the next-best thing. It helped renew my mushing confidence."

Osmar really did not enter the Iditarod thinking he was going to be able to win it after winning the Quest. He was meshing some of his father's dogs with his own. They were good dogs, but ordinarily not good enough to make his first-string. Some of those top dogs raced in the Yukon and were now on leave, resting on the Kenai.

The younger Osmar laughed when someone asked how much sleep deprivation one human body could stand by doing the two races in a row. He pointed out that sleep deprivation is part of his regular routine in the summer, too. "It's good training for the fishing season coming up," Osmar said.

With many eyes charting his progress, Osmar set off from Anchorage, heading to Nome to see if he could accomplish a miracle. At the least he wanted to acquit himself well. He did the latter. By placing eighteenth in the Iditarod that year, Osmar established a new milestone. He became the first musher to win the Quest championship and to finish in the money in the Iditarod in the same year. He did not contend for the lead in the Iditarod, but what he did altered musher and fan thinking: it was possible to do well in both races in the same year.

"I raised the bar," Osmar said.

Osmar kept mushing, raising his kids, and working as a commercial fisherman in the summer. He expanded his kennel and started leasing dog teams to beginning mushers who sought to run the Iditarod for the adventure. One year, not only did Osmar enter, but three additional teams of Tim Osmar dogs were in the event, plus a team belonging to his father. Osmar dogs could have held a trail reunion at a checkpoint, imagining they were back at the kennel.

"It's a ton of dogs," Tim Osmar said. "It's crazy, really. We had an army of dogs."

In 2008, he was committed to lead legally blind musher Rachel Scodoris along the Iditarod Trail. The plan was sidetracked when a fire threatened Osmar's Ninilchik home and other homes in the area and he fought the blaze trying to save the structures. While attempting to quell the flames, Osmar broke his right ankle and leg.

From the musher who had raced two long-distance races in one year, Osmar became a musher who could not manage any trail time in February or March of 2008. He spent the ensuing year healing and returning to full strength. In March 2009, Osmar was back in the Iditarod, fulfilling his commitment to guide Scodoris. Traveling close together, the duo faced down hellacious winds, bone-chilling temperatures, and reached Nome one after the other.

The completion of the race marked a different kind of two-pronged achievement — helping someone else cover the distance at their own pace — and simultaneously bouncing back from severe injury. Eight years had passed since Osmar conquered the Quest, and it was nearly a quarter of a century since he began competing. It was about time for Osmar to take another run at the Quest Trail. Another trophy would look fine in the living room, and after all, he still spent his winters training in the Caribou Hills. The dogs just might relish another go at the Quest's major summits.

CHAPTER TWENTY

SO CLOSE

"Rosebud, Eagle, American, King Solmon's Dome — each of these mountains left its mark on past Quests. They separated champions from the pack. They compelled the weak to quit."
— Brian O'Donoghue, *Honest Dogs*

2009   William Kleedehn's hardy dogs led the 2009 Yukon Quest to the base of Eagle Summit. If they could climb the steep pitch smoothly, his dreams might come true. At this late stage in the twenty-sixth annual race, Kleedehn could dare to hope that he might take command and capture his first victory in twelve tries.

Kleedehn had run well the entire way from Whitehorse. His dogs had sneaked past Jon Little in the night to claim the halfway gold prize in Dawson City and, although Little and Hugh Neff hung close, it seemed that Kleedehn's dogs were the ones to beat as they approached the final few hundred miles of rugged trail in generally benign weather.

Quest mushers were fortunate. In prior weeks, the entire region from the Yukon to Interior Alaska had been gripped by fearsome cold, the kind that made metal brittle. There were days of minus 50 F (-46 C) when mushers were wary of taking their teams on extended runs. Forget-about-it cold was one way to describe that intense air.

Yet, when the race began in Canada, warmer weather prevailed. There were no storms, only light snow occasionally. There were days of sunshine and temperatures even rising above zero. And, as promised by race officials, the trail was groomed better than it had been in recent races. Conditions were as favorable as they ever got on the Quest.

With 250 miles (402 km) remaining to the finish line in Fairbanks, Kleedehn had a two-and-a-half hour lead. Not insurmountable, but if nothing went wrong, comfortable. Everyone thought so, until by cutting rest and calling upon an energized team, Neff slashed Kleedehn's team's lead to three minutes leaving Central with 160 miles (258 km) to go. It was a risky move that could backfire, or a bold one that could win him the title.

Then abruptly, the race took a quirky turn.

Leaving Central, Neff got off the regular trail at Circle Hot Springs where the race briefly follows the road. But rather than quickly return to the trail, Neff mushed on the road for more than five miles (nearly nine kilometers). Kleedehn saw him and so did reporters covering the race. Neff did not believe that he gained that much of an edge, but race marshal Doug Grilliot slapped Neff with a two-hour penalty that had to be served at Two Rivers, the final checkpoint and a mandatory rest stop. Whether the mistake stemmed from brain-lock, fatigue, or something else, Neff would have been better off taking an extra two-hour rest rather than his tour of the highway. He said later that he had stayed on the road because he thought Kleedehn had done the same. Seeing "dog poop" was the trail sign he followed, Neff said. The poop alibi did Neff no more good than if he said he had been following Lassie.

The next challenge was Eagle Summit. Before tackling it, Kleedehn took a break at the Steese Roadhouse. He ate a steak and contemplated his place in the Quest universe. Neff and Kleedehn are friendly and share mutual respect. Kleedehn did not criticize Neff's *faux pas*, but instead expressed admiration for how Neff was keeping up with less rest. "His team is really amazing to me," Kleedehn said.

After more than 800 miles (1,287 km) of racing, Kleedehn said he felt the trail physically. "I'm a little bit bruised and battered, but I'm still here," he said.

Kleedehn was wise to fortify himself with that steak. He had no idea how much energy he was going to need to get through the next day. Racing with the burden of the penalty hanging over his head, Neff reached the base of Eagle Summit first and his dogs charged up the hill.

Kleedehn trailed, but felt good knowing he had a two-hour time bonus on Neff. Then everything went haywire. Kleedehn's team of frisky dogs, so full of run until then, took one look at the steep grade leading to the 3,685-foot (1,123-meter) summit and, much as Bruce Lee's sled dogs had in 1998, declared "No way."

Kleedehn's response was something on the order of "What do you mean, no way?" only with much more colorful language. Worse yet, the dogs became distracted by one of the great wild cards of life — sex. Until then, female leaders Breeze and Marimba and male leader Fajita had been totally reliable for Kleedehn, but then Breeze went into heat and the males surrounding her lost their minds. It was like a singles bar on a Friday night. Common sense went out the window as the males attempted to impress a female that gave off obvious signs of being interested.

Eagle Summit is just about the steepest incline on the Quest Trail. It requires narrow focus, intense concentration, and physical stamina to climb over the top, particularly when its finicky vicious weather pops up. Kleedehn did not need the aggravation of dogs with sex on their minds. He needed them performing in other ways. He was coping with a sit-down strike. He wanted the dogs to run. They refused. The terrain and the dogs' hormones conspired against him, but the result was the same. Kleedehn said, "I couldn't go backwards or forwards."

Along came Little, and his dogs also mushed onto the mountain. Kleedehn tried to convince his dogs to follow Little. No go. Kleedehn pondered turning back to Central to drop Breeze, definitely a distasteful chore.

Now Neff and Little led, and in a race where the weather had been tame, they dared hope to have an easy passage over Eagle Summit. It was not to be. As they approached the summit the weather deteriorated, and a storm blew in accompanied by high winds. They halted.

In a matter of minutes, with Kleedehn stuck at the bottom of the hill, to Neff and Little stuck near the top, the entire complexion of the race changed. "It was blowing really hard and drifting," Little said. "We were cold and wet."

Neff said he figured it was too good to be true that a dog team could make it through the Quest without violent weather. "It was like living in a fantasy world for a week and a half and then came Eagle Summit," Neff said. "For six to eight hours we were in a raging blizzard with no markers. It was pitch black. The dogs didn't know where to go."

There are several mountainous high points along the Quest Trail, but Eagle Summit is the most notorious, with the worst track record of shattering mushers' hopes. In 2006, mushers had to be air-lifted off the Summit. Past champ Frank Turner had his biggest trail nightmare on Eagle Summit. Vern Halter recalled dismal circumstances during unexpected hellacious weather on the hill. In the 1989 race, Halter said, he, Sonny Lindner and Jeff King got caught in 40 to 50 mph (64 to 80 kph) winds and turned back to a shelter cabin. Later, he saw another musher passing by bundled in so much clothing as to be unrecognizable. "I don't know if I've ever seen anything more miserable," Halter said.

It was just Eagle Summit exacting its toll.

Neff and Little were in the front, leading the Quest, with Kleedehn, their strongest competition, trapped behind them. Yet, they could not move away from him. They were shut down, too. At the Mile 101 dog drop on the Steese Highway, race officials stood around in sunshine, with the thermometer miraculously inching up. When weather isn't a factor, the run from Central to 101 can be made as swiftly as five and a half hours. Quest officials were unaware of the drastic conditions faced by Neff and Little, and they wondered where everyone was. When nobody mushed in after twelve hours, a snowmobile search was organized. Kleedehn was spotted at the base of Eagle Summit, but no one else was in sight.

Back at the Central checkpoint, Sebastian Schnuelle took his time getting back on the trail. He felt there was no chance to run down the trio of mushers ahead. Kleedehn, Neff, and Little had too much time on him, and were running teams too fast to catch. Schnuelle was fourth and he was okay with that. Not bad, he thought. He mushed out of the checkpoint more than eight hours after Neff and Kleedehn had departed.

Later, reporters informed Schnuelle that mushers had told them they thought he was the one to beat. He was astounded. "They did?" Schnuelle said. "I guess they knew more than I did. In Central, I had given up. I wasn't even in race mode. The summit changed everything."

That it did. The three mushers ahead of Schnuelle were stymied. Schnuelle set out from Central and first caught the frustrated Kleedehn. Schnuelle attempted to coax Kleedehn's dogs to the summit. He led the team partway up the hill, but they would not go on. Schnuelle mushed ahead, resuming his own race as he realized how close he was to Neff and Little. "I said, 'William, you are on your own now,'" Schnuelle said.

Brent Sass, the young Fairbanks musher, was the next to encounter Kleedehn. "It was on the steepest of the steepest part where he was stuck," Sass said. The men teamed up and at last Kleedehn's dogs went over the summit. But not before Neff and Little had moved on.

At one point, Neff disembarked from his sled and became his own lead dog in a whiteout. At the top, all of the trail markers had blown away. It was impossible to tell which way to go. Little caught up, the two men parked their sleds and searched for the trail for about ninety minutes in the dark, before declaring a rest break. They wiggled into their sleeping bags and napped for about five hours until daylight.

By then, Schnuelle had made up much of the time deficit and was close to the lead. After the news blackout on the leaders' whereabouts, Neff arrived at Mile 101 first and Little and Schnuelle came through within an hour. Sass and Kleedehn trailed by a couple more hours. Neff and Schnuelle were moving well. Little fooled the competition into thinking his team was just as strong, but his dogs were flagging. Eagle Summit, Little said, "was the pivotal point."

It was a whole new race.

"It's luck," Schnuelle said of his timing as he took over the lead. "It's pure luck. It wasn't even the wildest dream of my mind."

HOURS LATER, in mid-afternoon, it was sunny and clear on Eagle Summit. The wind died down, visibility was perfect. Martin Buser, his head filled with stories about the summit's past destruction of race optimism, crossed over the same terrain with his dogs zooming like race cars.

Far back after setting an early blistering pace, Buser was in a jolly mood as his team perked up. He was coming hard and could even joke about the conditions he faced on the summit. "I missed Eagle Summit," Buser said.

That's how easy it was for him. A little bit of cooperative weather makes all the difference.

CHAPTER TWENTY-ONE

FIRST THREE PEAT WINNER

"It's a tough race, over demanding country, it's often extremely cold, and you travel on primitive trails broken out only at race time. As a physical test, mushers give it five stars."
— Jeff King, *Cold Hands, Warm Heart*

2002-2004

Hans Gatt was the Quest's first dynasty. The Austrian transplant to the Whitehorse area became the first musher to win the Quest three times and he did so consecutively in 2002, 2003 and 2004. When Gatt took over the race he did so with a vengeance. After starting out as a sprint musher in Europe, and competing in the Iditarod, Gatt made the Quest his own personal party for three years, making him the top dog in Quest history.

Gatt, fifty, has a dashing persona. He is confident, but charming. With a full head of dark hair, an athletic body, and a few craggy age lines, he is as Hollywood-looking as anyone in his sport. There are only a few places in the world where one can live and have a chance to make a full-time living in dog mushing. Gatt knew that Europe was not one of those places.

When Gatt told his family in Austria what he wanted to do, everyone thought he had lost his marbles. That was then, and this is now. "Not anymore," he said of those doubting family members' sketchy belief in his sanity.

Gatt came to North America to develop his sprint-mushing team in the top races in Alaska, including the Anchorage Fur Rendezvous and the Fairbanks North American. He competed well for several years. Sprint-mushing competition was the showcase mushing event of the winter throughout the 1950s and 1960s in Alaska and remained popular throughout the 1970s, even after the Iditarod began. However, as the popularity of the Iditarod and the Quest soared and the adventure races attracted sponsors, interest in speed events declined.

"My goal had been to make a living," Gatt said. "But it became in sprint mushing that unless you were heavy into selling dogs, you couldn't do it."

So Gatt made the transition. No more twenty-mile races. Bring on the the 1,000-mile (1,609-km) races. At the time, Gatt lived in Atlin, British Columbia. In the 1990s he began training for long distances and moved to Whitehorse. He made his debut in the Quest in 1993 and finished a respectable seventh, but he didn't really enjoy it. Many racers who begin in the sport take up mushing as a hobby and enjoy backwoods camping trips. They travel long and slow and realize that the skills they pick up may well transfer to the Quest.

Gatt was coming from the other direction. He had been racing dogs short and fast and was not used to the long, long hours, extending into days, on the trail. While the others were like 10,000-meter runners going into the marathon, Gatt was like a 100-meter runner moving up to an ultra-marathon. A fit man, Gatt really was a marathon runner himself, so he understood the dynamic, but the shift was jarring.

"It was such a drastic change from sprint racing to the Quest and I didn't know anything about long-distance racing," he said. "I just wanted to complete it. That was never an issue, but after that I thought 'I'll never do that again.' And I didn't until 2002."

Still, Gatt knew he had to adapt if he wanted to stay in step with the times. He began racing the Iditarod and got used to tough trails, rugged terrain, and long races. Over time he grew to like the marathon events.

"My attitude had changed and when I came back to the Quest in 2002, I wanted to win it," Gatt said.

The 2002 race started in Fairbanks. Gatt was determined to forge a lead from the beginning. There was a solid forty-one-musher field that year, including past champions Frank Turner, Rick Mackey, Dave Monson, and defending champion Tim Osmar, plus hungry contenders William Kleedehn, Thomas Tetz and Peter Butteri. That was a high-quality crowd of mushers with experience on the Quest Trail, something Gatt lacked. Gatt had exceptional speed in his team, however, and cruised through the early stages past Mile 101.

"Right at 101, I made a big mistake," Gatt said. "I got lost on Eagle Summit. I lost a couple of hours. Those couple of hours I never really made up until the end of the race. I didn't want to make them up then. I just wanted to be with everybody."

The conservative strategy paid off. Of the mushers with big names who seemed likely to be the toughest to hold off, it was Butteri, a Quest veteran from Tok, Alaska, who had begun his competitive career with a last-place, red lantern finish, who proved to be the toughest to beat. Butteri was holding tough and leading beyond the halfway point in the Yukon.

Then Gatt turned his team loose and ran 75 miles (121 km) non-stop between Carmacks and Braeburn Lodge to take the lead. Butteri had completed a rest and was about to head back out on the trail when Gatt passed him. It was a critical moment. Butteri could not reel Gatt back in and Gatt beat him to the finish line by 1 hour, 23 minutes. The winning time was 11 days, 4 hours, 24 minutes.

Gatt had the good sense to finish about 5 p.m. in Whitehorse. Not only was it daylight, but the work day was just ending and fans poured into the street. A huge, cheering throng greeted the Quest's first European winner. "That was quite the special part of it," Gatt said. "I've never seen that many people at the finish line."

Tetz, Monson, and Kleedehn filled out the top five as Gatt collected $30,000 and decided long-distance mushing might yet be his thing. Osmar finished eighth the year after his own triumph.

Gatt returned to defend his crown, calling the 2003 event "an amazing race" characterized by extraordinary cold that year. When even mushers utter the words "extreme cold," it gets your attention. The lowest temperature Gatt experienced in that race was 61 F degrees below zero (-51 C). And that was after it was warm enough to rain at the start. "It was a crazy race at the beginning," Gatt said.

Most places that put up with frigid winters don't mind if there is a brief thaw. But people who mush dog teams hate rain. It is too warm for the dogs to race comfortably and the precipitation can wash away good trail. If the trail's top layer evaporates, sometimes a layer of ice or mud is left. The 2003 Quest saw a temperature swing of 95 degrees. Up and down, hot and cold. In the severe cold, it becomes a challenge for mushers to function at all.

"First of all, you have to move very carefully," Gatt said. "You don't want to make any stupid mistakes. I was running a lot next to the sled to keep warm. The dogs were great that year. The temperature was extremely cold for about a week. In the beginning of the race I was wearing just a ball cap on my head. In Dawson City, the temperature just dropped and the second half was just ridiculous."

When Gatt talks about "stupid mistakes" he is referring not only to getting lost on the trail, but also simple things like taking a glove off for a moment while feeding dogs. Naked flesh exposed to the air in severe cold does not present a pretty picture.

"I think everybody had some sort of frostbite in the race," he said. "I was lucky. I was pretty good with my fingers in the cold then. Not so anymore. I think they have been exposed too long. Now I'm kind of wimpy. Now, almost every training run I get out on, I freeze. I freeze my fingers. I freeze my toes. It's just getting old. It probably has something to do with age, but also with the exposure to cold weather for so long. I'm fifty and the last couple of years I've noticed a huge difference."

That new vulnerability to cold was not yet evident in the 2003 race where, by definition, Gatt functioned best of all because he won. After the temperature plummeted in Dawson City, what had been a close competition became a blowout. Gatt's dogs surprised even him by performing brilliantly in the second half of the race. They disregarded the cold and he handled the cold well enough to stay up with them. The team, human included, turned the race into a romp and Gatt took his second straight Quest title in a swift 10 days, 18 hours, 28 minutes. "Things just exploded and I ended up with a fourteen-hour lead," Gatt said.

An interesting aspect of the 2003 finish was that the top three placers were Europeans who had come to Canada to make a new home. Gatt was first, Kleedehn second, and Tetz third. Fourth was previous two-time champ John Schandelmeier.

Gatt left that fine field in the snowy mists behind him. Kleedehn took second in 11 days, 9 hours, 4 minutes. The gap between first and second was so large that Gatt had enough time to eat, drink, be merry and get a good night's sleep before the runner-up came into the finish chute.

The reception at the finish line wasn't as welcoming for Gatt this time because he arrived around 4 a.m., so his victory was a little bit lonelier.

Gatt's second win in a row was a first. He joined the company of John Schandelmeier and Charlie Boulding as two-time champs, but neither had accomplished their feat consecutively. When Gatt signed up for the 2004 race, he was going after a three-peat, the sports phrase popularized by Los Angeles Lakers coach Pat Riley when his team was chasing three National Basketball Association titles in a row.

It was not as star-studded a field as Gatt faced in his first win. Schandelmeir was giving it a go, as were Turner and Tetz. Michelle Phillips and Sebastian Schnuelle were two fresh faces in 2004.

ONE OF THE unknowns from a Quest perspective was Zach Steer. Steer grew up in an athletic family in Anchorage, Alaska. One sister, Becky, was an accomplished triathlete. Another sister, Rachel, was a U.S. Olympic biathlete in the Winter Olympics. Steer, who operates a lodge about 100 miles (161 km) from Anchorage with his wife, gravitated to mushing.

Steer was not a wealthy musher and shared a partnership in a kennel with another dog driver. They frequently alternated running the Iditarod and sometimes Steer surprised the top racers with his good finishes. In 2004, when it was his turn to run the dogs, he chose to enter the Quest, and Steer became Gatt's main competition.

The Iditarod is often run at a faster pace than the Quest. Steer went out quickly in the Quest and set a tempo that might have intimidated other mushers. When such a swift start is established by a musher, especially one whose capabilities are less known, top mushers must decide whether he is for real or a fluke — will he build an insurmountable lead, or will he tire and come back to the pack? Odds are the dogs will grow fatigued and be reeled in later, but there is always the chance that this will be the musher who can't be caught. Bruce Lee faced the same dilemma in 1998 with Andre Nadeau, as Gatt did in 2004 with Steer.

The two events turned out in almost the same manner. In both cases, the Quest veteran trusted his own instincts to run his own pace and to let the newcomer go. Lee overtook Nadeau and Gatt raced down Steer.

"Zach went out very fast," Gatt said, "but I never really got too worried about him. He had up to a three-hour lead at one point, but I didn't really let it bother me because at that point I had won the race twice. I knew what it took to win and I never believed that he could keep up that pace."

Gatt was right. He stuck to his own schedule and caught up to Steer by Dawson City. After that, it was the veteran who ran away with the title, winning in 10 days, 17 hours, 54 minutes. Steer hung on for second, roughly eight and a half hours behind Gatt. Veteran Dave Dalton recorded his best Quest finish in third.

By winning three times in a row, Gatt authored fresh Quest history. Not only were the consecutive victories a milestone, but Gatt also became the first musher to win three Quest titles.

"It was pretty exciting," Gatt said, despite mis-timing his finish-line arrival to show up late at night when fewer fans hauled their bodies out of bed to clap.

When a champion wins year after year an aura of invincibility surrounds him. He becomes so confident that it adds a new element to his capabilities. And competitors tend to regard him as unbeatable. It happens in all sports, but what also occurs in all sports is that nothing lasts forever. Champions do get replaced. They may age, get injured, or otherwise falter. Young talent rises.

Sometimes, winners even get bored and retire. Sometimes they look for new worlds to conquer. That was Gatt's deal. After overwhelming the competition and setting records in the Quest, no doubt in his mind establishing marks that would last for years, he turned his full attention to the wealthier paydays of the Iditarod. In 2005, he did not enter the Quest.

If Gatt could have glimpsed the future and seen that what he accomplished would be surpassed so quickly, he might not have been so hasty to take a vacation from the Quest. Five years later, with 20-20 hindsight, he believes he chose the wrong path by not trying for a fourth straight Quest win. "For some reason I decided not to run in 2005, which was a big mistake," Gatt said. "I'm sure I could have won that race. In hindsight, when I think back, I should have stuck to the Quest for all these years."

By 2009, Gatt was talking about retirement, but he entered the Quest and Iditarod anyway. He does think more about warm sunshine, though. After two winters helping Jamaican Newton Marshall prepare for the race, that Caribbean island became one of Gatt's favorite vacation spots.

Gatt banked the 2002, 2003, and 2004 titles, but by 2009 Lance Mackey had won four titles in a row, eclipsing Gatt's three-peat achievement. In 2009, Gatt returned to the Quest for one last hurrah. He was after a head-to-head match-up with Mackey. But Gatt knew he had lost his hunger. Winning or losing did not mean as much to him as it had in the past. It was one last Quest and out, for sure.

CHAPTER TWENTY-TWO

A LEGEND IS BORN

"I don't think there has ever been anybody like Lance Mackey." — Frank Turner

2005 Lance Mackey is the greatest winner in Yukon Quest history. He is threatening to become the greatest winner in Iditarod history. He wins with superior teams and superior strategy. He wins on a fast track and on a stormy track. He wins with grace, charm, and self-deprecating humor.

And he wins after doctors said he had no right to win, that he should not have had the strength, the will, and the determination to survive cancer. In some people's estimation, Lance Mackey should have been dead and buried years ago under the same hard ground his dogs run over. He is on the cusp of being regarded as the greatest long-distance musher of all time and he knows better than anyone that he is the luckiest man in the world just to be breathing.

The reign of Lance Mackey in the Yukon Quest began in 2005, but the improbable journey of Lance Mackey began well before that.

Mackey's father, Dick, helped Joe Redington start the Iditarod in 1973 and won the championship in a hellbent-for-the-finish-line sprint against Rick Swenson in 1978. His winning time was one second faster than Swenson's in the closest finish ever.

Lance Mackey's half-brother, Rick, won both the Iditarod and the Yukon Quest, so Lance grew up in a mushing family. "As I got a little older I decided I wanted to race dogs in the winter and fish in the summer," Lance Mackey said. "I thought that was the perfect combination because the people I know who were commercial fishing then were making a lot of money."

However, after some rudimentary mushing, he rebelled. As a teenager, he was more troublemaker than goal-focused young man. He was a self-described juvenile delinquent more likely to engage in risky business than to take risks in the wilderness.

He did not know what he wanted to do with his life, almost up until the time he fell ill. Ten years ago, Mackey lived in a tent on the beach in Kasilof, Alaska, and relied on a food bank for sustenance. Commercial fishing wasn't paying the way he thought it would. He was thirty by the time his interest in mushing was rekindled. It didn't hurt that neighbors included Tim Osmar, Dean Osmar, Jon Little and Iditarod musher Paul Gebhardt. They were a good influence.

By 2001, Mackey had about ten dogs, mostly castoffs from his father and Rick, and some of them even came from the dog pound. He used to give his children rides through the woods and he raced his dogs at a local sprint track. He convinced his wife Tonya that he might be able to make a go of racing, and that the first step was to breed better dogs.

Following family tradition, Mackey entered the Iditarod Trail Sled Dog Race in 2001. He had high hopes, but the race did not play out as expected. Mushers usually are run down, fatigued, often subject to catching the flu or even pneumonia as they push hard through sleep deprivation. Mackey felt lousy for a good portion of the race.

More telling, there was a lump in his neck. After completing the race, he visited a doctor and received frightening news — the lump was a malignant tumor. Mackey had throat cancer requiring surgery and chemotherapy.

The treatment was harsh. Not only was Mackey weakened and diminished by his cure, but there were two side effects that to some degree continue to this day. He lost his sense of taste and he cannot raise his right arm above his shoulder. At the time he was living in a mobile home with no insurance. Mackey was very sick and the radiation doses drained him.

What Mackey did have was time on his hands. During his recovery, he bonded closely with his dogs. He gave love and lapped up their love in return. Relationships developed with his huskies that boosted his spirits and the time invested with the dogs boosted the trust between man and animal. This was a critical period in Mackey's development as a musher.

"My taste buds were zapped by the radiation," Mackey said. "They're coming back. I've got some taste buds going now, but no saliva glands, no lymph nodes. Hell, I haven't got many teeth. The circulation in my hands and feet are bad.

"The surgery was on my right side. The mass was wrapped around the main muscle that controls my right arm. They had to take that out as well, which left two small muscles controlling my right arm, and in most cases those muscles aren't big enough or strong enough to function, to move your right arm. I couldn't lift it over my head. I still can't lift it over my head without the assistance of my other arm, pushing up on my arm. I have to watch my hydration. Because I have no saliva glands, I've got a water bottle all the time."

When doctors examined Mackey, the illness was somewhat advanced and it was a good thing he had not waited any longer to see them. After the debilitating treatments, they told Mackey he should be well enough to resume a normal life, but that he would not be able to mush again.

"That was probably the worst thing they could have told me," Mackey said, "because I'm not the kind of person to tell that I can't do something."

When Mackey decided to become an Iditarod racer he was embarking on a five-year plan. He thought it would take that long to become a contender. As soon as doctors said he wouldn't be able to do the Iditarod anymore, Mackey made plans to do the Iditarod. It was eleven months from surgery to the starting line and when the 2002 race names were called, Mackey's was among them. Race fans applauded his gumption, but some thought his presence was a mind-over-body trick. Mackey was not as well as he appeared to be. He still had a feeding tube imbedded in his belly.

"I couldn't eat because I had no teeth and that year, because of the radiation and treatments and all that stuff, I wasn't real active,"

For those who regard the Iditarod as the "Last Great Race," and a challenge that even at full strength can test the human spirit beyond endurable levels, Mackey seemed nuts. He knew he was not physically prepared, but throughout the year of his greatest trials in beating back cancer, entering the Iditarod served as a carrot.

"Mentally, that was what was keeping me going," he said. "It was something to get out of bed for every day. I had a goal and a plan and I wasn't going to let this thing take over my plans. In reality, I should have." He started, but could not finish the race. "I didn't have much money and it was a struggle for us to even make it to the race. Then, to scratch, that was the most difficult decision I've ever made. I felt I was letting down the sponsors that I did have and my family and myself."

Mackey raced 443 miles (713 km) to Ophir before dropping out. At least he proved to the world that he was still alive. In 2003, he took a wiser course. He lent his dogs to various mushers and focused on building his strength. In 2004, he and brother Jason each took a team to Nome in the Iditarod, both finishing in the top thirty.

"I was getting there," Mackey said. "But I still wasn't there. I'm still not up to par 100 percent, but mentally, my head, was 100 percent. My body was what was lacking. Physically, I'm maybe not as capable of doing some of the things that other mushers do, but I make up for it mentally."

What Mackey has never done is complain. He realizes that he is lucky to be alive and that even if he never got past finishing in the top thirty in the Iditarod he would be lucky. "I'm blessed," he said. "...I was lucky enough to even make it out of the operating room. By the time I got diagnosed and actually under surgery, it was in the late stages and they didn't know if I'd even recover, even pull out of it."

For lesser men, surviving and having the satisfaction of mushing again might have been enough. What neither Mackey nor anyone else could foresee was that he was about to become a phenomenon. Despite the setback of life-threatening illness, Mackey was on the verge of a breathtaking breakthrough. From a musher mostly known for the heritage of his last name, Mackey became the most popular figure in the sport and a symbol and inspiration for cancer survivors everywhere.

Mackey was friendly with Quest veteran Hugh Neff, and after the 2004 mushing season ended, Neff cajoled Mackey into trying the Quest. Neff, who is as talkative as a TV talk show host, kept repeating that it was a great experience and that Mackey should enter. "I had always wanted to run the Quest, too," Mackey said, "seeing the success Rick had. And it was another trail I hadn't seen. So, in 2005 we gave it a whirl."

At the time, Hans Gatt was the three-time defending Quest champ, the all-time winner in the event. But he skipped the 2005 event. The field was not deep, but it was highly competitive. Past champs Frank Turner and John Schandelmeier were entered. William Kleedehn, Gerry Willomitzer, Jon Little, Dave Dalton, Sebastian Schnuelle, and Neff were in the mix. Mackey was a wild card. His name was known, but his credentials were sketchy. At that point, he had received more attention for beating cancer into submission than he had for winning races.

What no one outside of the immediate Mackey family knew was that the dogs he and Jason ran in the previous year's Iditarod all belonged to Lance, so he could pool two seasoned teams of young dogs. Even Lance, though, thought they were at least a year short of their prime. "I had a nice team of young dogs, mostly just two and three years old," he recalled. "So we were just going to take a pretty nonchalant approach to it."

Although the names were well known, as were their track records, Mackey challenged some of the prominent Quest mushers at the right time. Their teams were past their primes, or not yet in them. They had difficulties on the trail. Mackey was just hoping to be competitive.

Kleedehn, Neff, Willomitzer, and Little led in the early going. Q & A sessions with Neff aside, Mackey really didn't even know the trail. "I was running with them, just kind of following their lead," he said. "Jon seemed to be the rabbit. He was out front and we were hop-scotching back and forth. I had a really, really good team and had a nice run into Dawson."

One minute Mackey was in third place, the next in fifth, the next he was second. Each team passed the other and then was passed back. "We were just leap-frogging," Mackey said, "and I felt I was as fast as anybody there. I just didn't really know how to race that race yet. I was learning as I was going. I was just following along. I didn't actually take the lead until we left Central."

As often occurs, crossing over Eagle Summit proved to be a test. Nasty weather caused Little problems, and Mackey passed him on the climb. As the race entered its final third, the newcomer was in the lead, on the lookout for a hard-charging Kleedehn.

"We left Angel Creek twelve minutes apart and twelve minutes apart with a team like Kleedehn's is not a comfortable feeling," Mackey said. Mackey was aware of Kleedehn's hovering presence all of the way into Fairbanks. The increased pressure of knowing that someone was ready to pounce if he made a mistake, kept Mackey alert.

"There were a hundred miles to go, but with a racer like him and his team, it was a little uncomfortable," Mackey said. "But you've got to be patient. I felt if I was in front and somebody's behind me they're going to have to push a little bit to catch me. And when they do catch me, I hope to still have a push left to pull away from them. That's what it was all about. I kept my cool and never tried to whistle my dogs up until I saw him, and I never saw him. I could tell he was right there. I just didn't see him."

Mackey's sixth sense was correct. Kleedehn kept pursuing and cut the final margin to eight minutes, but that gap was just a large enough distance for Mackey to maintain rather than put an extra log on the fire. Mackey's winning time was 11 days, 32 minutes. He won $30,000 in prize money and a million bucks worth of confidence. Mackey had gone from being just another racer to champion of the Yukon Quest.

"It was the changing point of my racing career," Mackey said. "We hadn't really been racing all that long and now I pull out a win in the Quest. People were shaking their heads and saying, 'Well, you got lucky.' There was a lot of that kind of talk . . . because Hans wasn't there, and he had won three years in a row. Everybody had expected Kleedehn to win and I kind of upset their little party. It was awesome for me."

It was awesome for anyone who heard Mackey's story. He rose up from poverty, overcame cancer, and recorded a remarkable feat. No one, not even Mackey, imagined the chain of events to follow that turned him into a folk hero.

CHAPTER TWENTY-THREE

MACKEY MAKES HIS MARK

"I owe it to my dogs for keeping me alive." — Lance Mackey

2006-2008 Lance Mackey is a slender man with long, dark hair who always seems to have a five o'clock shadow. He's got a sly smile, and the way he narrows his eyes slightly when he laughs gives the impression he knows he's getting away with something.

Perhaps he is.

If Mackey knows something you don't, it's because he's studied for it. All the mistakes he made as a young man on the trail, all the tough situations he's endured, have given him crucial wisdom, and turned him into a trail genius.

The 2005 victory in the Quest was a validation that Mackey was right to give competitive long-distance mushing a whirl, as he put it. The triumph also jump-started the most dominating stretch by any musher and kennel in the race's history. In 2005, Mackey showed up to participate in the Quest. By 2008, he was the king of it.

Mackey was happy that he won in 2005, but didn't appreciate negative talk at the water cooler. Some whispered that Mackey's win was a fluke; if Gatt had been present, Mackey wouldn't have won. There was great anticipation for the 2006 Quest. Mackey returned to defend his title and Hans Gatt returned after a year's absence. This time, the most recent champions would go head to head and have the company of William Kleedehn and veteran Dave Dalton at the front.

"After the first one, my confidence level built up," said Mackey, who retains many of his father Dick's New Hampshire speech inflections, despite having grown up in Alaska. "I knew my team was capable of winning. Everything was coming together in my program and I didn't care who was there or not. I felt I had as good a chance of winning no matter if Hans, Rick Swenson, or Martin Buser, or whoever was there. I felt I could compete with those guys."

If Mackey was feeling his way a little bit in 2005, following other mushers as he learned the trail, he was a different musher in his second Quest. The 2006 race did produce the anticipated duel between Mackey and Gatt. Mackey prevailed. His winning time of 10 days, 7 hours, 47 minutes established a new record on the Fairbanks-to-Whitehorse route. Gatt chased Mackey to the end, finishing 1 hour and 12 minutes back.

It was a satisfying win for Mackey. He quieted the whispers, ending the talk that had annoyed him. "Well, now Hans was there," Mackey said. "And Hans had excuses like, 'These two dogs didn't work out,' and 'I hauled a dog.' This and that. There was always an excuse. I had a mission that year and it was to take down the big guy. Hans was the big guy. I was out there to beat Hans and to show the rest of the field and the rest of the sport that the last year wasn't a fluke and that I earned what I did. So I really did need to pull off a second win."

At the same time Mackey was making his mark in the Quest, he was raising his profile in the Iditarod. In 2005, he finished seventh. In 2006, he finished tenth. His high finish once again enlivened the debate about a Quest-Iditarod double. Mackey was redefining the possibilities. Was the Quest-Iditarod championship double possible? Still, no one believed it.

"After my second win in the Quest, and finishing well in the Iditarod, that ... just sky-rocketed my confidence level in my ability and my team's ability," Mackey said. "That didn't mean I was going to win every race that I entered, but I knew I was capable of it."

In 2007, Mackey won his third straight Quest. His winning time of 10 days, 2 hours, and 37 minutes was a record. He defeated

Gatt by six and one-half hours. "Every race gets a little easier, or you learn more," Mackey said. "Now, for the second time, I've beaten Hans. And I had taken a four-hour detour. I had a twelve-hour lead 100 miles (161 km) from the finish line. It was a cruise-control type of run, but I got lost. I took a wrong turn."

It was the richest Quest ever. Mackey's first-place payday was $40,000. Mackey called his Quest run "flawless."

Mackey wasn't finished, though. He shocked the mushing world by winning the Iditarod in the same season, running most of the same dogs. He had accomplished the impossible.

"I've got a helluva group of dogs," he said.

There was no arguing with that.

Mackey returned to defend his Quest crown in 2008. Gatt sat out the race that year, but there was fresh competition. Ken Anderson, an Iditarod veteran, was Mackey's next-door neighbor on the outskirts of Fairbanks, where Mackey moved for better training. The prize money he was accruing enabled Mackey to start building a house — piecemeal. He and Tonya no longer lived in a tent.

Anderson had built his kennel into a perennial Iditarod contender and decided to take a shot at the Quest. In three years, Mackey went from incidental race contender to invincible race champion. He and his dogs beat back challenges from storms, frigid temperatures, high winds, and all comers on sleds. Anderson sought to grab his first major title and end Mackey's grip on the Quest.

Anderson's wife, Gwen Holdmann, had raced in the Quest. "She kept telling me how much tougher she was than me," Anderson said. "And I just always wanted to do it. I was always nervous about running the dogs in both races, wondering if it was too much for them. Then, when Lance did it and used almost all the same dogs, I thought more about trying it."

The temperature hovered around minus 40 F (-40 C) for the beginning of the 2008 Quest in Fairbanks. Anderson got off to a good start. He said the cold was a good slap in the face, but a mile shy of Chena Hot Springs, his sled's brake broke. "I came flying into the parking lot, weaving in and out, and bouncing off of cars," he said. If there was video, the slipping and sliding routine probably would have been a YouTube smash hit.

Anderson studied Quest history, past races, trail conditions, and picked his wife's brain for advice. He thought his best strategy was to run six hours and rest six hours, even if Quest checkpoints are not arranged conveniently for that game plan. The mileage between Quest checkpoints can tempt a musher into forgetting his original plans in the interest of pursuing comfort.

"It takes so much time that mushers typically stop in the checkpoints and take a major break," Anderson said. "And I tried to break from that."

On the trail, Anderson watched many other mushers break up their run-rest schedules into erratic patterns while he doggedly stuck to his plan. He had a good rhythm going and, by the time he arrived in Eagle, was in second place. "My team was coming on strong," he said.

Mackey was about twenty minutes ahead of Anderson going into Eagle, and they left the community together. It was a two-team battle. "I passed Lance right away, but he re-passed me and kind of walked away from me," Anderson said. "I started making some moves because we were going into Dawson for our thirty-six-hour layover. He had the slightly faster team, but instead of just following him, and following him, and essentially playing his game, I had to think outside the box."

The temperatures plummeted to minus 60 F (-51 C) at one point. "It was the coldest I'd ever run dogs in, so that was exciting," Anderson said.

Mackey says it is difficult to deal with such cold in the middle of a race. "The amount of clothing you have to wear to stay warm at those temperatures limits your ability to do things," Mackey said. "You have to really think about what you're doing. It's not as simple as getting out of bed and putting your socks and pants on. You've got to think about what your next move is. If you take off your glove to undo the zipper to your coat to get something in your inside pocket, well, that move right there could be the end of your race from the severe frostbite your fingers might get."

Then, to everyone's amazement, the weather did an about-face, and the temperature soared to nearly plus-30 degrees F (-1 C). Judging the sun to be too strong and potentially debilitating for his dogs, Anderson chose to rest and switched to running at night.

Finally, Anderson made a run for it, mushing for sixteen straight hours into Dawson. It closed Mackey's lead to about fifteen minutes prior to the mandatory layover. "I think we had the same speed in that run and just inadvertently rested the same amount on our stops even though we were resting 25 miles (40 km) away from each other and had no idea when the other guy was going to get up and go," Anderson said.

The mushers departed Dawson within minutes of one another. Mackey was mushing up King Solomon's Dome on a starry night without using his headlamp when he made a wrong turn and lost the trail. Anderson made the correct turn and moved into the lead, although he didn't know it at the time. "It took me a while to realize that he had gone the wrong way, but after about six hours or so I concluded that he was not on the trail ahead of me," Anderson said.

Anderson was three hours into resting at a makeshift camp at Scroggie Creek when Mackey pulled in, disappointed because of his lost time. The men did not talk much, but Anderson thought he had caught a break. Surely, Mackey was going to need to rest awhile. Anderson figured he was looking at a two- to three-hour lead, essentially a gift, because of Mackey's trail error.

When Anderson hit the trail, some 400 miles (644 km) from the finish, he thought, "I'm not going to see him for a while." Yet, only four hours later, Mackey appeared alongside him. "That really bummed me out," Anderson said.

Mackey's ability to catch up so easily was demoralizing. Anderson left Scroggie Creek with Mackey, but Mackey's dogs were fast enough to build small leads on each rest-run cycle. Anderson began cutting his rest times. He wanted to keep Mackey in sight, but he also wanted to avoid continuously catching up and then losing ground. He returned to his original flight plan.

"I decided I had to stick to my guns," Anderson said. "I pulled over when it started to get warm. He ran through the heat of the day. I thought, 'Man, he keeps doing this. Sooner or later I've got to catch up to him.' "

Mackey seems to have mastered the effects of sleep deprivation. He is aware that mistakes can be made, but he seems able to call upon a storehouse of energy that not all mushers have. Sometimes that means he pushes past normal fatigue into hallucination territory. He has seen and conversed with people who do not exist. Once, as he approached the Iditarod finish line in Nome, he saw stuffed animal heads mounted on the tops of every lamppost. In the Quest, he was mushing on the Yukon River — he thinks that's where he was — when he saw a lady standing alone in the snow beside the trail. This was the middle of nowhere. "I asked her what the temperature was," he said, "and she answered. Then later I asked other mushers if they saw her and, no, they didn't see her."

Another time on the Yukon River, Mackey was certain he saw a tree stump sticking out of the ice. "On top of the stump was a wooden canoe tied down," he said. "But there was nothing else around. I asked other people if they saw it and they didn't see it, so I just don't know if it was there or not."

About 250 miles (402 km) from the finish line, Anderson made a long run. He passed Mackey sleeping by the side of the trail, but the champ responded to his canine alarm clock — barking dogs. Roused, Mackey chased Anderson into Pelly Crossing. Anderson was first into the checkpoint, and a reporter asked, "What's it feel like to be in the driver's seat?" Anderson replied, "I'm not in the driver's seat." He knew Mackey was coming.

"I felt that I had the stronger, faster team throughout the whole race," Mackey said, "but Ken was making some unpredictable moves. He was like a shadow, and it was good for me to stay on my toes. I didn't feel it was a blowout at all, but I was a little more conservative knowing it was a two-person race at the end."

Going for the title and preferring to run through the night instead of the heat of the day, Anderson mushed sixteen hours non-stop to Carmacks. His dogs' power and speed thrilled him. But the feeling was brief. He looked over his shoulder and saw Mackey coming on the Yukon River.

"I thought I had put some distance on him," Anderson said. "Seeing him there it was obvious my plan didn't work. It was obvious he had a stronger team and it was pretty obvious that I was probably not going to win the race unless some miracle happened."

By informal agreement, the mushers decided to take a long break. No other mushers were close enough to make a charge and Anderson figured his best chance at victory was to rest his dogs for as long as possible. "I think we both kind of slept with one eye open," Anderson said of Mackey. "He's kind of a cagey guy."

Anderson was relieved when the break extended to nine hours. His goal was to stay within fifteen minutes of Mackey pulling into the Braeburn Lodge checkpoint for a mandatory eight-hour layover. But Anderson screwed up. At the campsite, he bent to the task of placing booties on each of his dogs' feet. Halfway through the task, Anderson was startled when — whoosh! — Mackey galloped away. Mackey realized that the snow conditions didn't warrant booty use. Anderson had wasted time with the booties and wasn't prepared to hit the trail. "I thought, 'Oh man, what am I doing?' He got about a fifteen-minute jump and I didn't need to give him that," Anderson said. "I could have left right with him and drafted off him."

Anderson's team made up time heading into Braeburn. He was behind by about the same amount of time that he had blown with the booties. He thought he could out-sprint Mackey over the final 100 miles (161 km). Mackey was driving eleven dogs, Anderson eight, but that disadvantage didn't worry the challenger as much as the trail. Officials warned of two overflow creek crossings, and when Anderson reached the first he had a devil of a time convincing his dogs that they really wanted to go.

"I had all kinds of trouble getting across," he said. "The dogs got tangled up and I had to drag them across. It was deep."

The water came up to Anderson's thighs and he got soaked. Anderson stood on the sled runners, balancing on one foot, trying to remove a boot and liner to wring it out as the dogs mushed on. He held up one bare foot at a time and once nearly tipped over the sled, requiring him to jam his naked tootsies into the snow to stop. The balancing act seemed ludicrous enough to be a candidate for America's funniest home videos.

This effort to dry out at full speed culminated just before Anderson reached the second creek. There, the water came up to around his knees, but was flowing much faster over a sheet of ice. Anderson was knocked over. Having perfected his offbeat drying method, Anderson tried it again. Mushing to within 30 miles (48 km) of Whitehorse, Anderson began to see spectators along the trail. As he mushed past, he shouted a question — how far ahead was Mackey? The unofficial response: about twenty minutes. Anderson was buoyed by the news, thinking that if his dogs got back in a groove they might catch the leader.

Anderson urged leaders Ochocco and Turtle to give everything they had. At the Takhini River Bridge, roughly 15 miles (24 km) from downtown, fans told him he trailed by five minutes. Because of curves in the trail, Anderson saw neither Mackey, nor signs of his headlamp. But abruptly his dogs seemed to run out of gas. "I just stopped and petted them," Anderson said. "I love them and sort of accepted that I just wasn't going to win, but we put on a good show." Anderson's challenge was over.

Mackey finished in 10 days, 12 hours, 14 minutes, his fourth straight victory, and collected $35,000. Anderson finished fifteen minutes behind him and made $25,000. At the finish line, the men shook hands and Mackey told Anderson, "I knew you were right there. I couldn't see you, but I could feel you."

Many spectators lined the incoming trail and filled up the downtown finish-line area. It was a good show for them, Mackey thought. "I'm going to assume there were a fair amount of people looking for Ken to take me down," he said. "People want to see a close race and occasionally they want to see a new face."

Mackey had posted a record fourth straight win in the Quest. A month later, he won the Iditarod for the second time in a row.

He was the toast of the North, the unbeatable musher collecting titles in 1,000-mile (1609-km) races at an unheard-of rate. *Sports Illustrated* ranked Mackey as the second-toughest man in sport— behind golfer Tiger Woods. A year later, the magazine bumped Mackey up to number one.

Although they saw his early potential, not even the people closest to Mackey believed he would become this dominant.

"He grew up in a dog lot and he was always good." Dick Mackey said. "His natural knowledge of working with dogs was always outstanding. He seemed to have that capability and that special knack. He grew up listening to all of the older generation talking about dogs, and he absorbed it. His dogs are his babies, but probably the greatest thing Lance learned in dog mushing was the absolute capability of his dogs. He learned his mental and physical limits and he had that capability of finding out the mental and physical limits of each dog." The elder Mackey is convinced that bonding with the huskies and setting the goal of racing again kept Lance going during the bleakest moments of his illness.

Brother Rick believes that the maturity and determination Lance has shown on the trail developed when he looked death in the eye. It made Lance stronger, Rick believes, and without that infusion of spirit, Lance could not have become the race conqueror that he has. "He made it through the cancer and decided he wanted to race dogs," Rick Mackey said. "By golly, he doesn't quit."

RICK MACKEY IS NO PSYCHOLOGIST, but he knows Lance. Lance agreed that Rick's analysis sounds right on.

"Absolutely," Lance Mackey said. "With the health issues I had, it was life-threatening and to pull through something like that and mush again, I'm just thankful to be alive. I guess I have a little bit more serenity. The dogs were part of the healing and my recovery. The fact that I was able to do things that people told me I would never be able to do again gives me satisfaction. They didn't know who I was and they didn't know what my attitude was."

CHAPTER TWENTY-FOUR

SURPRISE, SURPRISE

"Victory is won not in miles, but in inches. Win a little now, hold your ground, and later, win a little more." —Louis L'Amour

2009 Survival on Eagle Summit gave Sebastian Schnuelle the lead in the 2009 Yukon Quest. Mushers headed into the backcountry climb in one order and emerged in another. When they emerged, Schnuelle was ahead of William Kleedehn, Jon Little, and Hugh Neff. Once again, the course sorted out the vulnerable teams and the weather played havoc with race standings.

The object of any point-to-point race is to reach the finish line faster than anyone else. But external factors play a part. If the race is the Daytona 500, the driver must keep his car in one piece and not run out of fuel. If the race is the Olympic marathon, the runner must hydrate and pace sensibly. In the Yukon Quest, the musher must not only take care of his own body, but manage the needs and demands of a team of huskies — making sure they do not run out of fuel — and handle what the elements throw at him.

The race may not always go to the swiftest. It may go to the one that combines swiftness with smarts and the fewest mistakes. Neff had the fastest team, but he made a major boo-boo. Neff's two-hour penalty from race officials for running on the highway cost him dearly.

While the race — his race — unfolded on the Quest trail, Lance Mackey was busy preparing for the Iditarod. After four victories in a row, he was on vacation from the Quest, but it was not a relaxing break. By accepting a major payday from the Alaska National Guard to help a less-experienced musher train for the Iditarod, Mackey made the difficult choice to sit out the 2009 Quest. But he was antsy, itching to be out there. His mind wandered while performing ordinary tasks as he imagined his likely spot on the course.

In the middle of the Quest, as the mushers advanced from Dawson City into Alaska, Mackey hung out at a small weekend race near home, watching some of his inexperienced puppies run by a handler. "There's a nice little race going on and I'm not in it," he said of the Quest. He sighed.

Mackey is of medium height and probably weighs 150 pounds (68 kilos) under his bulky winter clothing, but he cast a large shadow over the Quest. As the race wrapped up, he materialized at the finish line on the Chena River, waiting like the other spectators to greet a new winner. Yes, he said, he missed the Quest. He was in the grocery store shopping and thinking about where he should be on the trail at that moment. While harnessing a team for training he pondered what type of strategy he would have employed in the Canadian wilds. He was around the house, but his mind was far away. Mackey definitely suffered withdrawal pains.

He grew more reflective. "If I finish thirtieth in the Iditarod, I'll be in the Quest for the next fifty years," he said. "I did want to win a fifth Quest in a row." It was too late for that second-guessing.

ON THE FINAL DAY of the Quest, mushers faced a mandatory rest in Two Rivers, the last checkpoint. With only forty-five miles to the finish line, most of the racing was over. Neff was first into Two Rivers, but he was being docked two hours for his goof on the highway. That dramatically altered the picture. After resting, Schnuelle could depart Two Rivers at 5:02 a.m. Neff could not leave until 5:37. Neff had forty-five miles to make up just over a half an hour. Everyone felt that was impossible, but Neff and his dogs weren't part of that discussion.

The sun was bright in Fairbanks that morning and the temperature was above zero. Church bells rang, and fans lined the finish chute under a big "Yukon Quest" sign on the frozen Chena as the first musher approached.

Schnuelle mushed hard from Two Rivers. He listened to the throbbing beat of AC-DC music on headphones and tried to resist turning around too often. He failed at the latter, constantly looking back while expecting Neff and his team to be eating up the trail. But Neff did not appear. Schnuelle crossed the finish line first, a dazed, but delighted winner.

"I knew he was close," the German-Canadian race veteran said. "I was pumping fast. It sure kept me on the edge of my seat. Every corner, I turned around and thought, 'So far, so good.' I knew Hugh had a lot of speed."

Neff and his dogs had the afterburners wide open. Steadily, he ate up the mileage. Neff hoped to catch sight of the leader, inspiring his dogs to run harder. But it never happened. Although Neff closed to within four minutes of Schnuelle's record-time winning pace at the end, he did it in a vacuum. Schnuelle's mark for the run was 9 days, 23 hours, 20 minutes, the first sub-ten-day Quest, and he collected $30,000. He broke Mackey's 2007 record by nearly three-and-a-half hours. The four-minute differential between Schnuelle and Neff represented the closest Quest in history.

"We never saw him (Schnuelle) over the last stretch," Neff said. "It's pretty funny that we ended up four minutes back. He was always around the next corner."

Schnuelle never really relaxed, but when he did not see Neff coming, he said, "The last couple of miles I thought, 'I guess it's going to be me.'" It was a good thing he never realized how close Neff actually was, Schnuelle said, because "I would have had a heart attack if I had seen Hugh. Thank God I didn't know that."

Schnuelle's wild hair was matted with sweat from the hard run in the sun and he jitterbugged around the finish chute, petting his dogs, accepting hugs from friends, and soaking in crowd applause. "I don't know if I've ever seen a happier man in my life," said former champ Vern Halter.

Schnuelle received a hug and a handshake from Hans Gatt who came to town to watch the end of a race he might have won if he stayed in it. "You really deserve it," Gatt told Schnuelle.

Schnuelle seemed shocked. When someone asked if he was going to celebrate with a few drinks he said he didn't think he could handle it. "If I have two or three beers I'll be dead," he said. "Maybe a Diet Coke." He seemed to need time to let his achievement sink in. "I'm the champion of the Yukon Quest," Schnuelle said tentatively, as if trying out the phrase for future use.

Little crossed the finish line third and partied with the fans, throwing them everything from Cadbury chocolate bars to chocolate chip cookies to fruits and nut mixes to summer sausage and cheeses. It was like Halloween. "Why not give the crowd something?" Little said. "I did everything I could to win, but I knew I wasn't catching anybody."

IN THE DARK, about twelve hours later, Martin Buser, who had rallied his team, and Michelle Phillips engaged in a flat-out race to the finish line, sprinting on the river. Buser prevailed for fourth and said every dollar earned would be useful during his campaign raising tuition money. "The last few hundred yards, I thought Michelle's boys were not in college yet," Buser joked. "I need it more than she does."

The difference was $2,000, prize money of $15,000 to $13,000. Kleedehn was sixth and won $10,000. In hindsight, he would have dropped the leader in heat before Eagle Summit, soon after he retired from racing.

Even if Schnuelle was too boggled to imbibe, Phillips wasn't. "I'm going to have a beer," she proclaimed.

Jamaican musher Newton Marshall not only beat the odds by finishing, but placed thirteenth and won $3,000. The best part of finishing was that Marshall could go indoors and warm up. But proving that memories are short, a few months later Marshall announced he planned to enter the Iditarod and train with Lance Mackey.

Schnuelle got some well-deserved sleep and when he woke he was still the champion of the 2009 Quest. A day and a half after his triumph, Schnuelle reflected on his future. He had capped his five-year plan with victory, had a welding shop in the Yukon, and owned a tour business providing sled-dog rides. "I thought, 'When I'm forty I'm going back to normal life,'" Schnuelle said. "I definitely will stay with dogs, but I definitely will gravitate towards the tour business." He smiled and said more firmly, "I'm the champion of the Yukon Quest."

Schnuelle planned to go out in style with this win, and did not plan to defend the crown. A few weeks later, he finished second in the Iditarod — behind Lance Mackey. Mackey electrified mushing fans by capturing his third straight Iditarod, overcoming stormy weather and severe cold to win handily. That gave Mackey wins in his last seven marathon races — four Quests and three Iditarods. If Schnuelle expected to fade off the radar of the competitive charts, Mackey wasn't going anywhere. Schnuelle might be out of the next Quest, Mackey planned to be in.

The winningest musher in Yukon Quest history found his true calling later in life than expected and found it the hard way. Initially, racing represented Mackey's quest to live. Then, he was on a quest to prove he is the best there ever was, even if he knows deep down that's not what it's all about.

The musher who beat cancer while proving doctors wrong made some of those same doctors his race sponsors. Mackey is a walking, breathing inspiration these days. People approach him on the street for autographs and tell him so. People write him letters and tell him so. People tell him their stories of hardships from cancer. They tell him, "Go get 'em." He has been doing just that. He has lived in the same mind and same body all of his years, the man once forced to live in a tent on the beach. It is a challenge to assimilate all of that adulation.

"It is kind of odd to me to have little kids coming up and telling me I'm their hero," Mackey said, "and people who have had cancer telling me that I'm an inspiration. It's kind of weird to me still. But in a way I think it's pretty neat because I am an example of someone who basically can go from near death to one of the top mushers in our sport. It has a lot to do with my personal attitude. I'm stubborn."

In no way does Mackey think of himself as invincible on the trail.

"I do the best I can with what I have," he said. "Expect the worst and hope for the best. It's all about the dogs to me. I want my team to speak for itself. I don't have to brag about my team. I want people to know they (the dogs) love what they do. I'm proud of what we've accomplished. But I honestly feel that we're not done yet. We're just getting started. I'm still motivated. I'm realistic enough to know that I'm not going to win all the races. That would be absurd to even think it's possible. But it's not absurd to think that I have a good shot at every race I do enter. I can't say how long this is going to continue as far as my abilities. My body is pretty beat up. But mentally I'm fine and I thank God for that."

The trophy case at Lance Mackey's household near Fairbanks is filling up, but overflow will be handled just fine. Each bauble of gold or silver represents a moment well lived and for Mackey that is the most important thing of all.

APPENDIX
Yukon Quest Champions, 1984-2009

Year	Winner	Time	Prize Money
1984	Sonny Lindner	12 days, 0 hrs, 5 mins	$15,000
1985	Joe Runyan	11 days, 11 hrs, 55 mins	$15,000
1986	Bruce Johnson	14 days, 9 hrs, 17 mins	$15,000
1987	Bill Cotter	12 days, 4 hrs, 34 mins	$15,000
1988	David Monson	12 days, 5 hrs, 6 mins	$20,000
1989	Jeff King	11 days, 20 hrs, 51 mins	$20,000
1990	Vern Halter	11 days, 17 hrs, 9 mins	$20,000
1991	Charlie Boulding	10 days, 21 hrs, 12 mins	$25,000
1992	John Schandelmeier	11 days, 21 hrs, 40 mins	$29,837
1993	Charlie Boulding	10 days, 19 hrs, 9 mins	$25,000
1994	Lavon Barve	10 days, 22 hrs, 44 mins	$20,000
1995	Frank Turner	10 days, 16 hrs, 20 mins	$15,000
1996	John Schandelmeier	12 days, 16 hrs, 6 mins	$25,000
1997	Rick Mackey	12 days, 5 hrs, 55 mins	$30,000
1998	Bruce Lee	11 days, 11 hrs, 27 mins	$30,000
1999	Ramy Brooks	11 days, 8 hrs, 27 mins	$30,000
2000	Aliy Zirkle	10 days, 22 hrs, 57 mins	$30,000
2001	Tim Osmar	11 days, 13 hrs, 38 mins	$30,000
2002	Hans Gatt	11 days, 4 hrs, 22 mins	$30,000
2003	Hans Gatt	10 days, 16 hrs, 28 mins	$30,000
2004	Hans Gatt	10 days, 17 hrs, 54 mins	$30,000

Year	Winner	Time	Prize Money
2005	Lance Mackey	11 days, 0 hrs, 32 mins	$30,000
2006	Lance Mackey	10 days, 7 hrs, 47 mins	$30,000
2007	Lance Mackey	10 days, 2hrs, 37 mins	$40,000
2008	Lance Mackey	10 days, 12 hrs, 14 mins	$35,000
2009	Sebastian Schnuelle	9 days, 23 hrs, 20 mins	$30,000

APPENDIX
Yukon Quest Finishers, 1984-2009

Abrahamson, Ed (1997, 1999)

Adam, Ross (1995)

Aldrich, Ron (1984)

Amundsen, Suzan (1994, 1996, 2002)

Anderson, John (1989)

Anderson, Ken (2008)

Andreonne, Tony (1986)

Atkinson, Rick (1985, 1987, 1988)

Ballard, John (1988)

Barb, Steve (1989)

Barnum, Dick (1989)

Barron, John (1994)

Barve, Lavon (1994)

Baureis, Bruno (2002)

Beisch, Benedikt (2007)

Bearup, Stan (1985)

Beattie, Richie (2006, 2007)

Bennefit, Braden (2002)

Bennett, Jim (1985)

Benson, Tom (2002, 2004, 2007)

Berry, Jack (1992, 1999, 2000)

Bicknell, Deborah (2000)

Blanford, Tony (1999, 2000)

Boily, Marc (1987)

Boivin, Kyla (2001, 2003, 2007, 2008)

Boulding, Charlie (1989, 1990, 1991, 1992, 1993)

Bouton, Jeff (1992)

Bowers, Doug (1991)

Bowers, Pete (1985)

Braun, Trevor (1997)

Bridges, Jim (1985)

Britten, Jean-denis (2008)

Brockman, Shannon (2002)

Brooks, Ramy (1993, 1999)

Buetow, Eric (1985)

Burmeister, Aaron (2007)

Buser, Martin (2009)

Butcher, Eric (2004)

Butteri, Peter (1989, 1991, 1992, 1994, 1996, 1999, 2000, 2002)

Bybee, Russ (2007)

Cadzow, Jay (1993, 1995)

Capot-Blanc, Adolphus (1986)

Cameron, Scott (1989)

Carroll, David (1997)

Carroll, George (2000)

Carroll, Larry (1998, 1999, 2000)

Hagan, Rusty (1998, 2000)

Hall, Wayne (2002, 2006, 2009)

Halter, Vern (1988, 1989, 1990, 1991)

Halvorson, Ty (1988)

Hanes, William (2007)

Harris, Doug (1996, 1998)

Hayden, Jack (1984, 1985)

Hendrick, Jim (1991, 1993, 1995, 1997,
    1999, 2000, 2001, 2002)

Hermann, Sepp (1999)

Herscher, Alain (1996)

Hibbs, Don (1995)

Holder, Bob (1988, 1989, 1990, 1995)

Holdmann, Gwen (1998)

Hopkins, Ed (1993, 1994, 1999, 2001,
    2005)

Humphreys, Pecos (1984)

Hutchinson, Doug (1993)

Jayne, Mike (2007)

Johnson, Bruce (1984, 1985, 1986, 1993)

Johnson, Larry (1987)

Jordan, Fred (1989)

Joy, Phil (2008)

Kaduce, Dan (2003, 2004, 2008, 2009)

King, Jeff (1984, 1985, 1986, 1987, 1989,
    1990)

King, Michael (1996)

Kirkvold, Keith (1998)

Kleedehn, William (1990, 1993, 1998,
    2001, 2002, 2003, 2005, 2006, 2007,
    2009)

Knott, Christopher (2002)

Kogl, Dennis (1985, 1988)

Korner, Beat (1991)

Kublin, Jim (1992)

Kuzyk, Gerry (1994)

Lee, Bruce (1986, 1988, 1989, 1991,
    1998)

Ledwidge, Ann (2008)

Ledwidge, Peter (1999, 2000, 2003,
    2004, 2005)

Lesh, Andrew (1997, 2000, 2001)

Lindner, Sonny (1984, 1986, 1989,
    1991, 1992)

Liss, Shirley (1984, 1985)

Little, Jon (2005, 2009)

Louden, Jerry (1997, 1998, 1999, 2000,
    2001)

MacDougall, Brian (1994, 1998)

Mackey, Brenda (1998)

Mackey, Lance (2005, 2006, 2007,
    2008)

Mackey, Rick (1996, 1997, 1998, 2002)

Mahler, Gene (1991)

Mahoney, Keli (2002)

Mann, Jeff (1992, 1993)

Marin, Marcel (2004)

Marshall, Newton (2009)

Massicote, Martin (2003)

Maurer, Mike (1989)

May, Joe (1985, 1986)

May, Mark (1994, 1996, 1997, 1999)

McAlpin, Bob (2007)

McLeod, Darwin (1990)

Miller, Jimmy (1991)

Milne, Bruce (2000, 2001, 2003, 2004)

Milne, David (2003)

Mitchell, John (1985)

Mitchell, Lorrina (1984, 1988)

Monson, David (1987, 1988, 2002)

Moore, Becca (2009)

Moroney, Diana (2002)

Mowry, Tim (1990, 1992, 1993, 1994, 1995, 1997, 1998)

Nadeau, Andre (1998)

Neff, Hugh (2000, 2002, 2003, 2005, 2007, 2008, 2009)

Nelson, Jamie (2002)

Nelson Sr., Louis (1998)

Nelson, Sam (1993)

Nicolier, Eric (2000)

Njootli, Stanley (1996, 1999)

Nordlum, Chad (2002)

Nordlum, Lucy (1992)

O'Donoghue, Brian (1998)

Oeschlaeger, Jim (2001)

O'Farrell, David (1997)

Oleson, Dave (1998, 2000)

Osmar, Tim (1986, 2001, 2002)

Palfrey, Warren (2009)

Palkovitch, Walter (1998)

Peep, John (1992, 1993, 1994)

Peep, Mike (1995)

Persons, Kate (1988, 1989, 1990)

Phillips, Michelle (2004, 2006, 2007, 2008, 2009)

Pinard, Catherine (2003, 2004)

Pinkham, Bill (2002, 2008, 2009)

Poage, James (1988)

Poage, Marc (1988, 1990)

Randall, Tom (1988)

Reitan, Ketil (1989)

Reiter, Jim (1988, 1990, 1994)

Riley, Gerald (1984, 1988)

Robertia, Colleen (2009)

Romenesko, Randolph (1991)

Rorabaugh, Darren (1997, 2000)

Rosser, Ron (1985, 1986, 1988)

Rudolph, Jon (1985, 1986)

Ruh, Heidi (1991)

Runyan, Joe (1984, 1985)

Russell, Philippe (2000)

Salter, Ed (1987)

Sam, Wilson (1984)

Santucci, Paddy (1994, 1996, 1998)

Sass, Brent (2007, 2008, 2009)

Sawatzky, Dave (1987, 1989, 1990, 1991, 1992, 1993, 2002)

Schandelmeier, John (1986, 1987, 1988, 1990, 1991, 1992, 1994, 1996, 1997,

1998, 1999, 2001, 2003, 2004, 2005, 2007)

Scheer, David (1989, 1991)

Schletner, Tonya (1991)

Schmidt, Karin (1987)

Schnuelle, Sebastian (2004, 2005, 2006, 2007, 2009)

Schwandt, Michael (1986)

Seekins, Ralph (1989)

Seibold, Dean (1986, 1987, 1994)

Shank, LeRoy (1987)

Shields, Mary (1984, 1986, 1988)

Sleightholme, Mark (2009)

Smith, Larry (1989, 1990, 1994, 1995)

Smyth, Cim (2000, 2001)

Stamm, Mark (1988)

Steer, Zack (2004)

Stewart, Bill (1995, 1996)

Steyer, Bill (1998, 2001, 2002, 2003)

Stoppenbrink, Norman (1993)

Strong, Jim (1988)

Studer, Crispin (2004)

Sutherland, Harry (1984, 1985, 1986, 1989)

Sutton, Iris Wood (2009)

Swanguarin, Kris (1996)

Swenson, Kathy (1986, 1987, 1988, 1994)

Taylor, Alistair (1996)

Taylor, Paul (1990)

Tetz, Thomas (1998, 1999, 2000, 2002, 2003, 2004)

Thomann, Peter (1990)

Thomas, H. Connor (1991)

Tingey, Ralph (1986, 1987, 1988)

Tucker, Kathy (1989)

Turnbough, Kevin (1984, 1987)

Turner, Frank (1984, 1985, 1988, 1989, 1990, 1991, 1992, 1993, 1995, 1996, 1997, 1998, 1999, 2000, 2001, 2003, 2004, 2005)

Tweddell, Luc (2009)

Varigas, Francois (1986, 1987, 1989, 1990)

Wade, Roy (1993)

Wardlow, Jim (1987, 1988)

Weiner, Martin (1986)

Whiton, Susan (1987)

Wiget, Thomas (1996)

Willomitzer, Gerry (2004, 2005, 2006, 2007)

Wilson, Jim (1989, 1991, 1994, 1995)

Wintter, Rick (1990, 1994)

Wright, Amy (1998)

Wycoff, Regina (2006, 2007)

Yuill, Senley (1984)

Zielinksi, Raif (1997)

Zirkle, Aliy (1998, 1999, 2000)

Zirngibl, Dieter (1995, 1996)

AUTHOR'S SOURCE NOTES

PERSONAL INTERVIEWS

Suzan Amundsen

Ken Anderson

Lavon Barve

Kyla Boiven

Charlie Boulding

Jean-denis Britten

Ramy Brooks

Martin Buser

Josh Cadzow

Kathy Chapoton

Bill Cotter

Dave Dalton

Bob Eley

John Firth

Hans Gatt

Doug Grilliot

Wayne Hall

Vern Halter

Frank Hauze

Jeff King

William Kleedehn

Mike Laforet

Bruce Lee

Sonny Lindner

Jon Little

Jason Mackey

Dick Mackey

Lance Mackey

Rick Mackey

Newton Marshall

Kathleen McGill

Dave Monson

Hugh Neff

Brian O'Donoghue

Tim Osmar

Michelle Phillips

Joe Runyan

June Ryan

Stephen Reynolds

Tamra Reynolds

Colleen Robertia

John Schandelmeier

Sebastian Schnuelle

Mark Sleightholme

LeRoy Shank

Tania Simpson

Thomas Tetz

Frank Turner

Roger Williams

Aliy Zirkle

NEWSPAPERS AND PERIODICALS

Anchorage Daily News Archives
Fairbanks Daily News-Miner Archives
Yukon Quest media guides

BOOKS

The Best of Robert Service, Robert Service
Cold Hands, Warm Heart, Jeff King
Yukon Quest, John First and Jurge Hampel
Honest Dogs, Brian O'Donoghue
Jack London Illustrated, Jack London
Klondike: The Last Great Gold Rush, Pierre Berton
Murder on the Yukon Quest, Sue Henry
Running North, Ann Mariah Cook
Racing the White Silence, Adam Killick
Yukon Alone, John Balzar
Yukon Quest: A Photographic Journey, Brian O'Donoghue

READING RECOMMENDATIONS
FOR SLED DOG RACING FANS

JON VAN ZYLE'S IDITAROD MEMORIES
30 Years of Poster Art from the Last Great Race®
Illustrated by Jon Van Zyle, stories by Jona Van Zyle
$9.95

IDITAROD CLASSICS
Tales of the Trail Told by the Men and Women Who Race across Alaska
Lew Freedman
$14.95

MORE IDITAROD CLASSICS
Lew Freedman
$14.95

FATHER OF THE IDITAROD
The Joe Redington Story
$19.95

HONEST DOGS
A Story of Triumph & Regret from the World's Toughest Sled Dog Race
$14.95

IDITAROD DREAMS
A Year in the Life of Alaskan
Sled Dog Racer Dee Dee Jonrowe
$14.95

IDITAROD FACT BOOK
A Complete Guide
to the Last Great Race®
Edited by Tricia Brown
$14.95

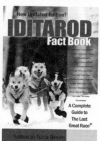

ONE SECOND TO GLORY
The Alaska Adventures
of Iditarod Champion Dick Mackey
Lew Freedman
$16.95

SLED DOG WISDOM
Humor & Heart-warming Tales
from Alaska's Mushers
Edited by Tricia Brown, illustrated
by Tom Nixon
$4.95

SPIRIT OF THE WIND
The Story of George Attla
Legendary Sled Dog Sprint Champ
Lew Freedman

ABOUT THE AUTHOR

Lew Freedman is the former sports editor of the *Anchorage Daily News*. He lived in Alaska for seventeen years and has visited the Yukon Territory many times. He lives near Chicago with his wife, Debra.

Major sporting events covered by the author:
Winter Olympics, Summer Olympics
Super Bowl
NFL Playoffs
NCAA Final Four
World Series
Kentucky Derby
Preakness Stakes
NBA Playoffs
NCAA track and field and cross-country running championships

Major sporting events covered in the North:
Arctic Winter Games
Iditarod Trail Sled Dog Race
Great Alaska Shootout
Top of the World Classic
Midnight Sun Baseball Game
World Eskimo Indian Olympics
Mount Marathon Race